WINDSOR GREAT PARK

The Walker's Guide

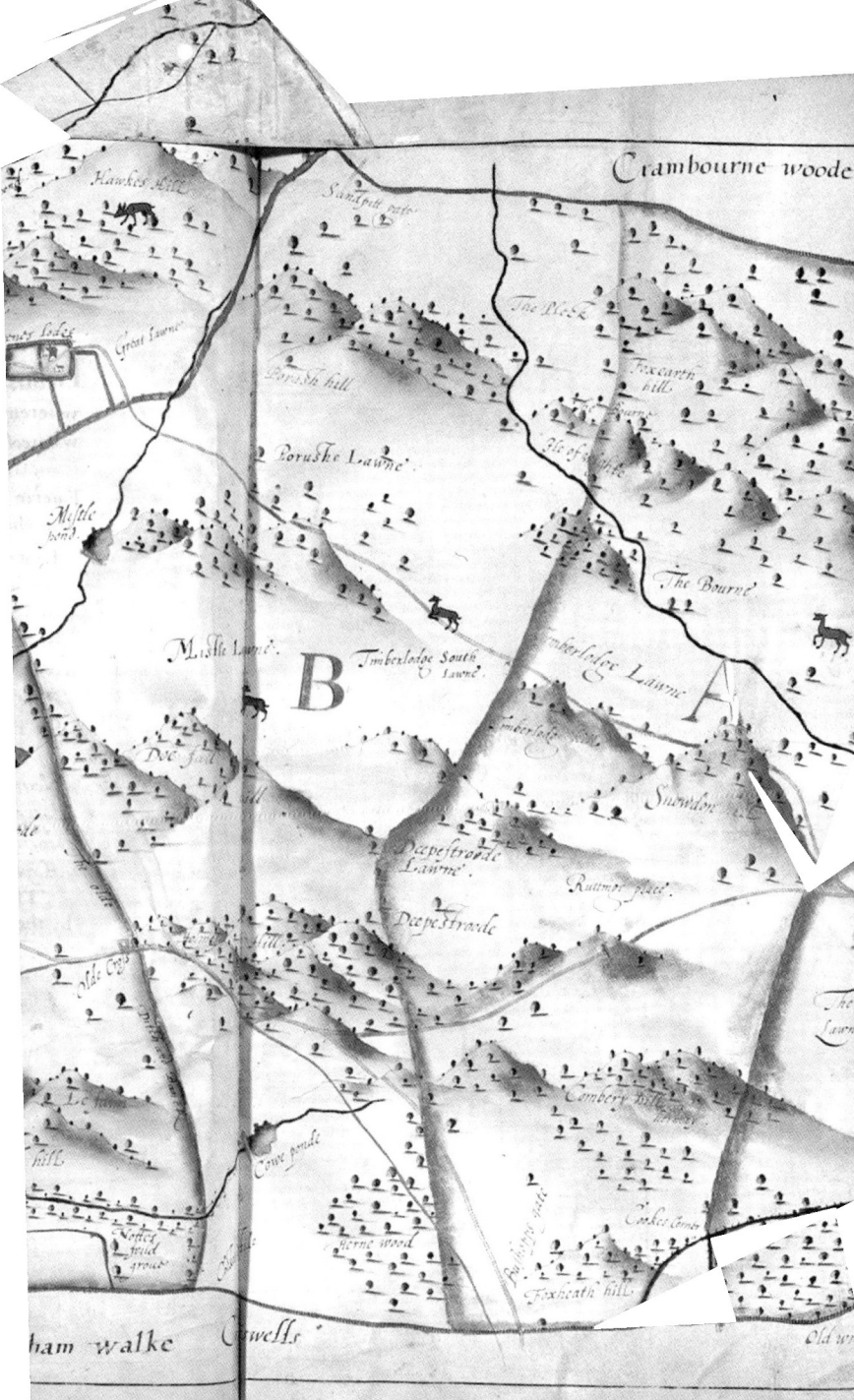

IN THE SAME SERIES

Richmond Park: *The Walker's Guide*

Hampstead Heath: *The Walker's Guide*

The Thames from Hampton to Richmond Bridge: *The Walker's Guide*

The Thames from Richmond to Putney Bridge: *The Walker's Guide*

Bute: *A Guide*

West Surrey: *Walks into History*

ENDPAPERS

John Norden, *Survey of the Honor of Windsor*, Table IV, The Great Park, 1607.

Front end papers: the southern section. Back end papers: the northern section. North is to right.

John Norden (c.1547-1625), born into a Somerset gentry family, was a surveyor and cartographer. His notebook of 1623 lists no fewer that 176 manors surveyed, many more than once. In 1600 he was appointed surveyor of crown woods and forests in southern England, and in 1605 he acquired the surveyorship of the Duchy of Cornwall. In 1607 Norden published *The Surveyor's Dialogue*, an attempt to persuade landowner and tenant alike of the value of a proper survey. It ran to three editions. Fees for surveys varied greatly and were sometimes augmented by gifts. We do not know how great was the fee for the survey of the Honor of Windsor, which contained numerous tables, but we do know that in addition to a fee, James I gifted him £200, equivalent to about £18,000 today, so he cannot have done too badly.

Norden produced extensive works on various counties. His most important was on Middlesex, the first English county map to mark roads. Norden was also responsible for introducing a grid-reference system, hierarchies of place and a key to symbols used on a map. When John Speed produced the first published atlas of the British Isles (his celebrated *Theatre of the Empire of Great Britaine*) in 1611, he used Norden's maps of Surrey, Sussex, Middlesex, Cornwall and Essex. *The Dictionary of National Biography* credits Norden with 'producing enduring images of English landscape that must have shaped the views which generations had of their homelands.'

WINDSOR GREAT PARK
The Walker's Guide

David McDowall

with sketch maps & line drawings by
Angela Kidner

COVER: *Windsor Statue*, Charles Sharland, 1912.
© TfL Reproduced courtesy of London's Transport Museum

First published by David McDowall
13 Cambrian Road, Richmond, Surrey TW10 6JQ

© David McDowall 2020

The right of David McDowall to be identified as the author of this work has been asserted by him in accordance with the Copyright, Design and Patents Act 1988

British Library Cataloguing in Publication Data
A catalogue record for this book is available from the British Library

ISBN 978-1-8381980-0-8

Designed and typeset in Monotype Octavian and Formata by Peter Moore
Printed in Hong Kong
The Hanway Press Ltd, London & Lion Production Ltd

'A true conservationist is a man who knows that the world is not given by his fathers, but borrowed from his children.'

John James Audubon 1785-1851

Contents

Introduction		page 14
Walk No. 1	*Moat Park and Cranbourne*	18
Walk No. 2	*Around the Village*	42
Walk No. 3	*Around the perimeter of Norfolk Farm*	55
Walk No. 4	*Virginia Water*	73
Walk No. 5	*Cumberland and Royal Lodges*	95
Walk No. 6	*The Deer Park and the Long Walk*	121

The Gardens of Windsor Great Park 138
    Eric Savill 139
    The Savill Building, the visitors' centre 142

The Savill Garden 143

The Valley Gardens 148
    Where to walk? 155; The Punch Bowl, 155;
    The Rhododendron Garden, 156;
    The Hydrangea Garden, 70;
    The Heather and Dwarf Conifer Garden, 157;
    The Pinetum, 159; The Totem Pole, 162.

    Plants of the Valley Gardens 167
    azaleas, 167; Wilson's Kurume Fifty, 169;
    camellias, 170; conifers, 172; hydrangeas, 177;
    magnolias, 178; rhododendrons, 178.

The political landscape 185

The ecological and economic landscape 203

George III and Agriculture 217

Nathaniel Kent, Charles Townshend and the Flemish and Norfolk farms	220
Longhorn cattle	226
Royal and regimental goats	229
Index	232

Maps

Windsor Great Park overview	17
Walk No. 1 Moat Park	19
Walk No. 1 Cranbourne	30
Walk No. 2 Around the Village	43
Walk No. 3 Around Norfolk Farm	56
Walk No. 4 Virginia Water	78
Walk No. 5 Cumberland Lodge and the Royal Lodge	96
Walk No. 6 The Long Walk and deer park	122
The Valley Gardens	150

Illustrations

Moat Park: detail of John Norden's map of 1607	22
Moat Park: detail of John Vardy's map of 1750	23
The Moat Island Cottage	24
The Moat Island Cottage converted to dwellings	25
A staff cottage designed by George III	25
Flemish Farm	28
Cranbourne Lodge	36

The Chief Guide, Lady Baden-Powell, at the World Guide Camp, 1957	41
George IV at Sandpit Gate	47
Henry Wise's map of the Great Park, c. 1712	50
Norfolk Farm	60
Tented camp on Smith's Lawn, 1915	65
Canadian Forestry Corps base camp	66
Canadian Forestry Corps tree felling in the Great Park	66
High Bridge	71
The summer house on China Island	80
Virginia Water drained, showing old pond head	84
The Fishing Temple	92
The Flying Barn	98
Detail of Henry Wise's map, c. 1712	100
The Great (later Cumberland) Lodge	102
How the Royal Lodge looked in George IV's day	105
The Whitehall (Holbein) Gate	110
Harvesting crops beside the Long Walk	111
The original gates, lodges and cottages at the Royal Lodge	116
Felling the elms of the Long Walk, 1943	129
The south side of Windsor Castle, c. 1719	132
Dragoons on the Review Ground	135
George V and Lord Baden Powell review the Boy Scouts, 1911	136
Sir Eric Savill in attendance as the Queen plants a tree	140
Clearing the ground for the Savill Garden	144
Clearing 'Upper Burma' in the Valley Gardens	149
Re-planting a rhododendron from Tower Court	157
The Wedding Party – Qagyuhl	163
Masked dancers – Qagyuhl	164
Annotated sketch of the totem pole motifs	165
Ernest Wilson	169
George Forrest on his first arrival in China	180

George Forrest after his escape	182
Forrest's team of plant collectors	183
Roger of Trumpington	194
A mature standard oak	210
Boxed heartwood of oak	211
Coppice sequence	212
Pollard oak sequence	213
A lapsed pollard	214
Don, George III's Merino ram	217
The Suffolk Plough	222
The Norfolk Plough	223
The improved Long Horned cow	226
Billy, the regimental goat	230

Acknowledgements

THE ILLUSTRATIONS

The illustrations have been reproduced by kind permission of Lucy Archer, p.116; the Berkshire Record Office, pp. 25, 98, 102, 132, 222, 223; The British Library, pp.24, 71; The Crown Estate Commissioners, pp.23, 28, 60, 84, 111, 129, 140, 144, 149, 157; Roger Cullingham, pp.65, 136; The Guide Association, 41; London's Transport Museum, cover; The Royal Botanic Garden, Edinburgh, pp.180, 182, 183; The Director and the Board of Trustees of the Royal Botanic Gardens, Kew, p.169; The Royal Collection Trust/ © Her Majesty Queen Elizabeth II 2020: endpapers, pp.22, 36, 50, 80, 88, 100, 110.

THE WORDS

Much less has been written about Windsor Great Park than about the Castle. Two books, however, stand out. William Menzies' *The History of Windsor Great Park and Windsor Forest* was published in 1864. Menzies was Deputy Surveyor for the Great Park during the middle years of that century. His book is authoritative and beautifully illustrated with fine photographs. It is an important resource. The definitive account, however, is to be found in Jane Roberts, *Royal Landscape: The Gardens and Parks of Windsor* (Yale, 1997). I could not possibly have produced a walker's guide without having this wonderful encyclopaedic work constantly at my elbow. If you find yourself completely smitten by the landscape of the Great Park, as I have been, splash out on this book. It is a real treasure-chest which you will never regret buying. Contained within this ultimate oracle, is the definitive collection of illustrations of the Great Park, and those who have been important to it. A shorter and less researched book, Clifford Smith's *The Great Park and Windsor Forest* (New Romney, 2004) also contains facts of more local interest. As for the Savill and Valley Gardens, if you seek something more substantial than the official publications currently available at the Savill Visitors Centre, obtain a copy of Lanning Roper, *The Gardens in the Royal Park at Windsor* (Chatto and Windus, 1959), still not hard to find.

THE PEOPLE

Every time I embark on a book, I am reminded of our great indebtedness to helpful librarians. When I first used research libraries over 50 years ago, I was warned that librarians came in two categories, those who believed in making books available to interested readers and others, of whom in those days there was still a substantial number, who believed in protecting books from anyone stepping across the library threshold. Today the latter, thankfully, are a real scarcity. In preparing this book I have encountered great helpfulness from the staff of the London Borough of Richmond upon Thames library service, the London Library, the Royal Horticultural Society library, the National Library of Scotland, and the British Library. I should like to mention by name librarians whose assistance went beyond the call of duty: Jane Roberts of the Royal Library, Windsor and Karen Lawson who both went out of their way to facilitate the provision of pictures from the Royal Collection; Linda Burtch of the Sault-Ste. Marie Library, Ontario, who went to considerable trouble to procure pictures for me. In Edinburgh, Leonie Paterson of the Royal Botanic Garden enthusiastically helped me find suitable pictures from the George Forrest photographic collection, while at the Royal Botanic Gardens in Kew, Julia Buckley furnished me with a portrait of Ernest Wilson within a couple of hours of my telephone call.

Others who have helped include Lucy Archer, who generously provided me with A.R. Bowling's photos of her father's short-lived gate lodges for the Royal Lodge, Henry Cadogan, James Cathcart, Roger Cullingham, Jack Langton, and David Piachaud. I am particularly grateful to two of the principal officers of the Great Park, Bill Cathcart, the former Superintendent, and the late Mark Flanagan, the Keeper of the Gardens. Both of them were generous with their time and their encyclopaedic knowledge of the landscape and its flora. They both looked at my typescript for errors of fact and judgement. In addition, Bill Cathcart wrote a generous commendation for this book, for which I am indebted to him. If errors remain, I am solely responsible.

Three people closer to home made the book what it is: my dear wife, Elizabeth, who checked each walk on foot and also edited the book with great thoroughness. Angela Kidner also walked the ground of each walk prior to preparing the maps and also the sketch of the Totem Pole. As usual, her maps are both clear and beautiful to behold. Deborah Wolton has kindly allowed me to use her drawings of coppice and pollards yet again. Finally, Peter Moore designed the book with the skill for which he already enjoys a fan club of which he is largely ignorant: the many people who tell me how exquisitely my efforts have been presented in printed form. Without the contribution of all the above, this book would have been the poorer.

Introduction

This book is intended to help you explore Windsor Great Park in all its astonishing variety of landscape. It is laid out as a series of walks, whereby you may visit virtually every part of the Park accessible to the public. It is my hope that you will discover, as I did, that it is much richer than you might realise on cursory acquaintance. For this is one of the great landscapes of England, containing one of the finest collections of veteran trees anywhere in the world, with traces of its medieval uses, and also the hallmarks of power: the Long Walk and the other avenues that stretch across the landscape.

Alongside man's historic interaction with the landscape, however, I hope you will also become conscious of the changes in terrain and its flora. Geologically speaking, one may divide the Great Park into three: the northern plain, largely clay but ending in the northern outcrop of chalk on which the castle stands; a central belt of loam; and the south-eastern hills made up essentially of sand. This geology determines, of course, the kind of flora one will find growing on the different soils. The first two are landscapes full of nutrients and there is little difference in what will grow. But the south-eastern part is markedly different, an acidic landscape on which acid-loving plants predominate. It is here, of course, that the Savill and Valley Gardens are located, for that very reason. Most of the exotic plants flourish here on account of the soil.

I have designed several of the walks to defy modernity, with its tarmac roads, and to re-awaken in the mind's eye, the medieval dimensions of the park, or rather parks, for the Great Park today is an aggregation of several estates, and more than one deer park. So I hope you will tolerate my obsession with trying to spot the medieval 'pale', or boundary, of the Great Park, still visible, in some places obviously so by the veteran oaks growing along it, and in other places barely perceptible, just a faint ripple on the ground, where 700 years ago there was a substantial bank with fencing.

It is impossible to walk around the Great Park without noticing that the speed limit is 38mph. How on earth did the Crown Estate Commissioners arrive at 38mph? It seems that at the time of decimalisation of the currency in the early 1970s, it was anticipated that miles would be officially abandoned for kilometres. The Great Park was to have a speed limit of 60kph. Until the time when kph officially replaced mph, however, the signs gave the equivalent, 38mph. Somewhere some official must still be eagerly awaiting instruction to repaint the signs in kph.

It is impossible to prescribe walks either in the Savill Garden or in the Valley Gardens. You should wander in both where your fancy takes you. So I have written background notes to both gardens and some of the more notable exotic plant species to be found in them, and also the sometimes hair-raising exploits of those who went in search of them.

I have also added two short pieces, one on the 'political' landscape, i.e. Windsor Forest and the deer parks that formed Windsor Great Park, and a second on the ecological and economic landscape, to indicate the ecology and function of this kind of terrain over the centuries. One or two other short background pieces will be noted in the list of contents, too long to integrate into any particular walk, but which I thought would still be of interest.

You are free to ramble across all the publicly accessible areas of the Great Park, courtesy of the Crown Estate Commissioners charged with safeguarding this landscape for future generations. I have two principal pleas. First, never stick to the routes I prescribe if your inclination is to follow your nose. Personal whims are more fun than prescriptions and should be followed. The second is to ignore anything in this book which you cannot spot on the ground or which becomes tedious. In this last respect I am conscious that at times I have been carried away by the (to me) fascinating history that attends some of the landmarks here. You can avoid tiresome stops on your walk by skimming the text of each walk beforehand, and alerting yourself to some of the background information and anecdotes I could not resist including. So, just get out there and enjoy it.

David McDowall
Richmond, March 2007; revised, October 2020

Key to the overview

 CLOSED AREAS

Ⓐ CRANBOURNE TOWER
Ⓑ THE COPPER HORSE
Ⓒ THE VILLAGE
Ⓓ FOREST LODGE
Ⓔ THE ROYAL LODGE
Ⓕ CUMBERLAND LODGE
Ⓖ THE OBELISK
Ⓗ JOHNSON'S POND
Ⓙ TOTEM POLE
Ⓟ CAR PARKS

Windsor Great Park: overview

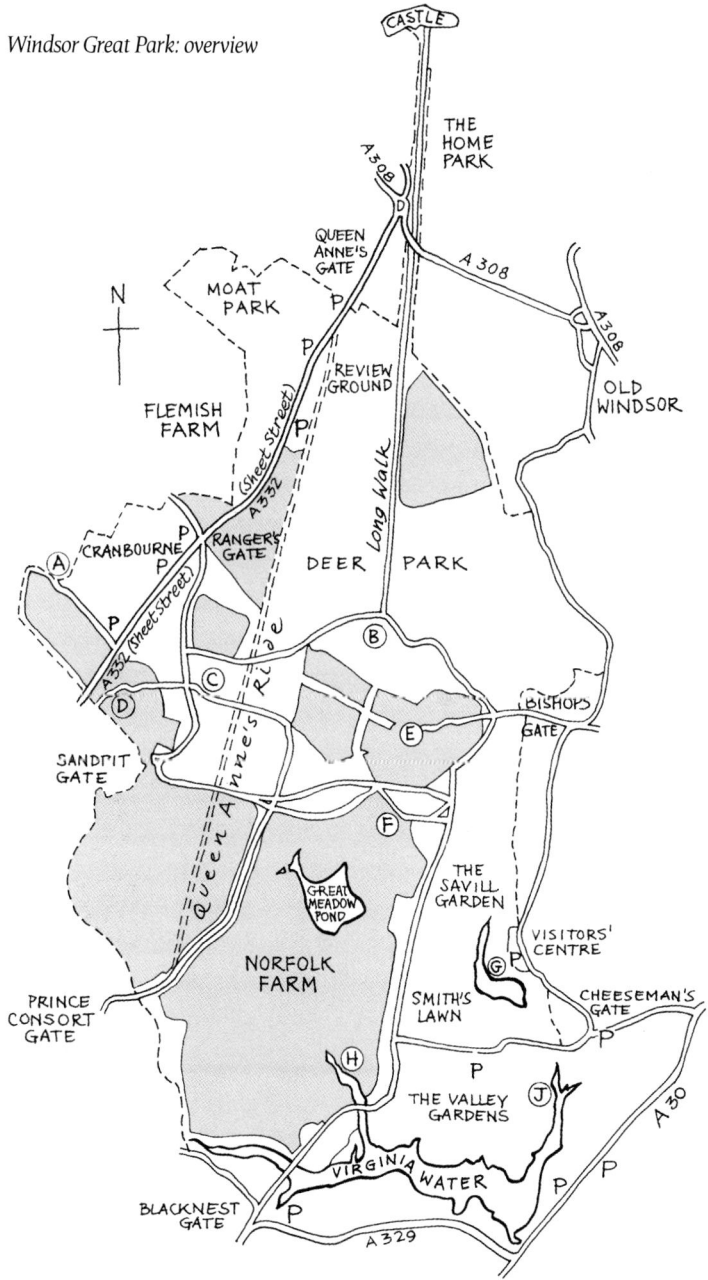

WALK 1

Moat Park and Cranbourne Rails

Distance 8km: 2½ - 3 hours

BEFORE YOU WALK

Both on this walk and on Walk No. 2 considerable reference is made to the park pales. These were deer park enclosures, earth banks topped with fences of oak palings. In the middle ages Moat Park was entirely separate from Windsor Great Park, and had its own enclosure, traces of which remain evident but are frequently hard to spot. Today, the line of the old pale can more easily be traced by veteran oaks still growing out of the pale banks (but, confusingly, there are plenty of other veteran oak trees in the landscape). Elsewhere the bank has been totally erased. Although they have been marked on the sketch maps where they are still discernible, these pale banks are now often barely ripples on the ground, so please do not waste time getting frustrated trying to detect something you are unable to see. It will only spoil your enjoyment of the walk. Please accept that they are there, even if you cannot quite discern where they lie. By tracing them regardless of the modern landscape, one starts to visualize the historic landscape in the mind's eye, and modern tarmac starts to seem what it really is, a recent and distracting interloper on an ancient terrain.

Moat Park has a shadowy history. It was a distinct enclave within Windsor Forest from sometime in the Middle Ages, when it briefly passed into the hands of Henry VI, probably in the

MOAT PARK AND CRANBOURNE RAILS 19

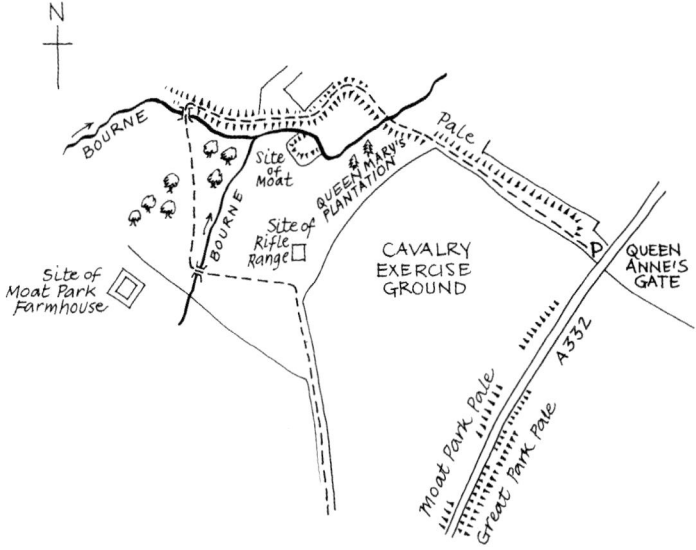

1420s or 1430s. It was presumably cut out of Windsor Forest as an authorised clearing. Such clearings, usually for agriculture and known as assarts, were increasingly frequent occurrences during the Middle Ages. Moat Park, however, was probably a deer park at the outset but it may also have contained other livestock. There is no evidence that the land here was ever put under the plough. By the early seventeenth century the herd of 280 fallow deer (see p.192) was being looked after by a Mr Staffordton, probably a descendant of a William Staverton, a deer-keeper to Edward IV, who held Moat Park in the 1470s. Until the industrial revolution, the same career was usually followed in each family for generations.

Start: at the car park on the west side of Queen Anne's Gate (immediately on the right of the road as one enters the Great Park from Windsor on the A332). Note: You may break this

walk into two distinct parts if you wish. Cranbourne may be explored as a second distinct walk by picking up the walk at the car park opposite the Ranger's Lodge (p. 29).

Start on the formal path, and count 90 paces. You should reach the 90th pace as you approach a small kink to the right in the path. On your right you should see a couple of young oak trees, the second next to an enormous old tree stump.

These trees and the veteran stump, are growing on the eastern pale of Moat Park. A few metres further north the pale turns and runs westwards almost parallel with the path you are on. The two converge. The northern pale also has a few old oaks, but also plenty of elm suckers. Most significantly there are the substantial remains of the bank and ditch that once bounded the northern edge of the deer park, dug (or even re-dug) in the fifteenth century (see p.195). As for elm suckers, they grow for a few years until killed by Dutch elm disease, carried by the elm bark beetle. They perish when they reach the height at which the beetle flies. They virtually never survive into maturity, yet they are a frequent presence in old 'relic' hedgerows. The only chance for the English elm in the long term is that the beetle mutates, so that it ceases to kill off the tree on which it lives.

To your left, running alongside the A332 you may note the ragged line of veteran oaks running southwards, more of the eastern pale of Moat Park.

Continue walking along the formal path for about 400 metres. Abandon the track where it branches left just in front of the plantation.

Before mounting the embankment straight ahead, you will see just to the right of the footpath you are about to leave, one metre or so on its right, the last ripple of the old pale.

So, mount the embankment, or bund, and continue walking.

The plantation on your left, Queen Mary's, dates from 1924, so it is still young. Compared with self-sown woodland, such plantations tend to acquire character and charm only when they mature. In an age of instant gratification, one is reminded to take the long view.

Pause on top of the concrete culvert. This marks the eastern side and almost the north-eastern corner of Stag Meadow, an open field stretching west and southwards.

You will be wondering about the bund and the culvert. Following torrential rainfall in October 1993 the Bourne, which takes water draining off higher ground to the south-west, flooded parts of Windsor to a depth of 1.5 metres. The bund was built in 1996 to prevent a repetition.

Continue along the bund, beside the football ground, but pause when you reach the corner of the football perimeter fence abutting your path.

The football ground on your right occupies a corner of the meadow granted to the local footie club by George V in 1911. He was preoccupied with the unfitness of British manhood and made Crown land available for public sport. His obsession was vindicated on the outbreak of war when so many of the enlisted proved physically weedy, indeed to the surprise of a number of their German adversaries.

On the open ground on your left lies the heart of Moat Park, and this is where you need to use all your imagination. The moat and its island were where there is now a clump of brambles and the dead remains of a tree. The last vestiges of the moat are now intersected by the present course of the Bourne and are no longer visible except as disturbed ground, which one can just discern as

1 MOAT PARK AND CRANBOURNE RAILS

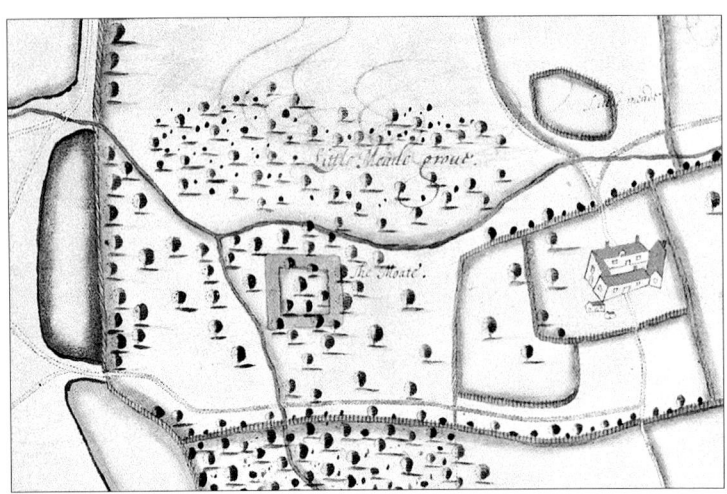

A detail of John Norden, Survey of the Honor of Windsor, Table V Moat Park, 1607, showing the square moat at the confluence of the two feeder streams of the Bourne, and the farmstead to the south (just beyond the land now publicly accessible). North is to the left.

slight depressions in the vicinity of the bramble clump. Originally the Bourne seems to have passed close to the moat and must have fed it, but its route has clearly been altered, possible in the effort to drain this low-lying and therefore permanently wet ground.

Unfortunately we do not know its origins or early owners. Yet in the Middle Ages the island probably boasted a house. Moated homesteads tended to belong to small feudal owners. These were working establishments integral within the land use pattern of the time, unlike the castles of great magnates, which usually stood apart and distinct. Moats first appeared as a building style in about the mid-twelfth century and enjoyed their greatest popularity in the years 1200-1325. Many moats did not fully surround the buildings they purported to protect. They often merely ran along the frontage and flanks, providing virtually no protection at all. It is possible that moats fulfilled the function of

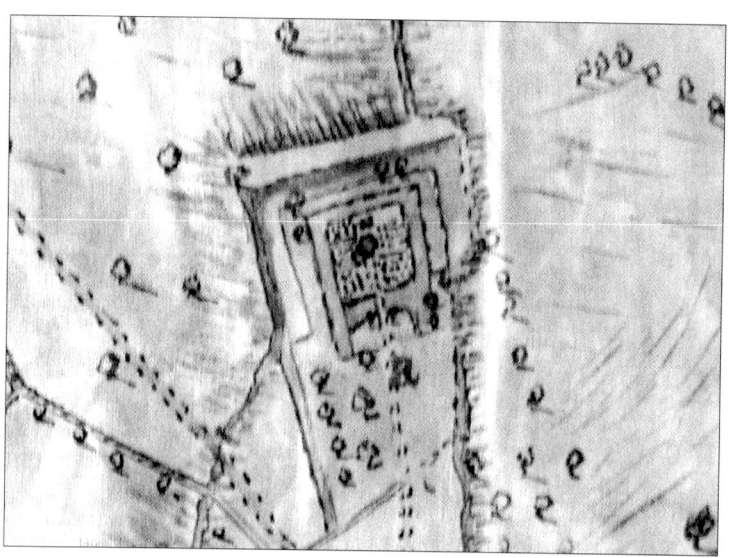

A detail of John Vardy's map of the Great Park, 1750, showing the Cottage and the configuration of water channels around it. North is at the top.

making the driving off of livestock harder, or helped protect the family from marauders. More probably, however, these moats were status symbols, like a handsome façade and generous front garden today, suggesting the property of persons of substance. The moat was still clearly depicted on Norden's map of Moat Park, dated 1607.

The site was adapted by the Duke of Cumberland (see p.73), who had been appointed ranger of the Great Park in 1746, on his return south from his victory at Culloden (p.95). He built a *cottage orné*, set in a small garden surrounded by water, presumably the old medieval moat. It was an Arcadian picnic place to which Cumberland and his coterie could resort. Cumberland turned to Christopher Gray, who had taken over his father's famous nursery in Fulham, for plants. Gray sent him a substantial variety, including bladder-nutt (*Staphylea pinnata*)

The Moat Island Cottage, *built by the Duke of Cumberland. The Bourne is on the right. F. Vivares after Thos. Sandby, c.1754.*

a recent discovery in the American colonies which produced handsome dark foliage, laburnums, different roses, honeysuckles and jasmines, Cornelian Cherries and 'cherry plums of Virginia'.

We are given some idea of what the Cottage looked like by Dr Richard Pococke, one of the most remarkable travellers of the mid-eighteenth century. Pococke had visited Thebes in Upper Egypt and also bathed in the Dead Sea to test a Pliny statement about the specific gravity of the water, something few others had tried (and if you have since tried, you will know why you will not repeat the experiment). Yet, insatiably curious, he also bothered to explore Britain and Ireland. He visited Windsor in 1754 and included Cumberland's island in Moat Park:

> '.... it is on a pond, with a cutt made round the island, on which a room is built in the figure of a Greek cross, with a couch on each side of the four parts of the cross; behind it, covered with trees, is a kitchen, &c. The Duke often comes here and spends an hour or two, and sometimes dines.'

Left: The Moat Island Cottage after its conversion into two staff dwellings. Another storey has been added to the structure, and the interior was cunningly split into two. Right: This staff dwelling, designed by George III himself, is probably how Stag Cottage looked. Both illustrations from William Pearce, A General View of the Agriculture of Berkshire *(1794). Pearce was Nathaniel Kent's admiring nephew.*

The Cottage was left as it was after Cumberland's death (1765), then converted in 1793 into a couple of semis, for two park keepers and their families, but demolished in 1896. One must conclude that all these activities, including re-routing of the Bourne, fatally damaged the original medieval site.

Continue along the bund, after 150 metres passing through a gap made by the bund in the hedgerow and fence.

The hedgerow line is at least 400 years old, but possibly a good deal older. On your right stands Clewer parish cemetery, with its chapel. Immediately on your right, against the hedgerow running up to the cemetery wall, stood Stag Meadow Cottage, another park keeper's house built in 1793, demolished in the 1920s. It took its name from the open meadows on your left, containing Moat Cottage and the surrounding pastures, through which the Bourne runs.

Watch out for the concrete footbridge across one of the two principal Bourne tributaries ahead of you on your left. Descend from the bund, cross it and take the path half left. After 100 metres you will cross a ragged avenue of oak trees, the second very incomplete line of oaks growing out of the ripple (presumably an old hedgerow bank) which you will cross.

This avenue was standing in the mid-eighteenth century. It is difficult to be sure whether this planting was the work of Cumberland or predates him. It was certainly planted after 1600. Most of Stag Meadow, as this area is known, was supposedly never put under the plough, but one can see that the landscape has nevertheless been substantially tampered with, to drain the land as well as to ornament it. This avenue may have lined a drainage ditch, since silted up. You may notice yourself crossing other depressions of silted-up drainage channels. It is probably on account of its generally damp condition that this ground always remained meadow rather than arable, but drainage was still important for livestock grazing.

After another 100 metres turn left on reaching the rough path, crossing a small bridge over another tributary of the Bourne.

Two fenced enclosures stood on your right, just beyond the present boundary hedgerow, in 1607, one of them containing some of Moat Park's farm buildings around a courtyard, for by now it had ceased to be a deer park.

Make for the right hand end of the loose clump of ancient oaks straight ahead.

At the left end of this clump, where it approaches Queen Mary's Plantation, a miniature rifle range was established at the time of the First World War and was demolished after the Second. It cannot have been a thing of beauty – they never are – its only traces now being disturbed ground.

Veer right on reaching the cycle track, turn right and follow it.
The track marks the eastern extremity of Stag Meadow. Beyond it, the wedge of land between this track and Sheet Street Road (A332) is known as the Cavalry Exercise Ground (discussed at the end of this walk, p.40).

On your right you will pass Swan Pond.
This pond acts as a valve on this tributary of the Bourne, which takes water running off Flemish Farm, on your right and Cranbourne, where you are heading.

As the ground rises, you enter a small grove, 'the Clump', with principally mature trees on your left, planted in the 1820s. On your right, on the side of the gully a cluster of young oaks is growing. Some of these oaks are approaching the age at which, before the industrial age, they would have been felled for use in housing, etc. Oak 'maidens', trees neither coppiced nor pollarded (see p.210), were usually harvested after 30 years or so, when they had acquired a diameter of about 30cm (12 inches). Any tree greater than 35 cm demanded significantly more labour on account of its weight. Beams cut with an adze from 30cm diameter oak trunks were adequate for domestic house building.

As you emerge from the grove and start to descend downhill, you will be able to see through the hedgerow on your right a couple of small woods on two hill tops.
The near right hand hilltop is Star Clump, planted around 1700. It seems to have acquired its name from the 'union-jack'

Flemish Farm, as it appeared in Nathaniel Kent's agricultural proposals for the Great Park, 1791.

cuts through it. Left of it, and further off, stands the wood on top of Bromley Hill, an eighteenth century plantation. In 1600 neither hilltop was planted. The 'Old Lodge' stood on the crest of Bromley Hill and its grounds, covering the whole summit around it, were empaled. Both clumps stand among the fields of Flemish Farm.

With his passion for improved farming George III (for more, see p.217) commissioned a leading agricultural exponent of his day, Nathaniel Kent, to design a farm on the lands of Moat Park in 1791. Flemish Farm is Kent's response, laid out in 1793 (for more on Kent and his farming methods, see p.220). The lower part of Moat Park remains publicly accessible because it was deemed too wet by Kent's drainage expert to be worth converting to arable land. Half a century later, the Prince Consort did what he could with the 240 acres of arable and another 160 acres of pasture. Gorse and fern were removed, fields re-arranged and the original buildings replaced with a new and commodious homestead. Waterlogged land had remained a fundamental impediment to productive agriculture, not only here in the Great Park but throughout Britain. In the early 1840s, Josiah Parkes devised a novel system of 'under-draining', by putting newly mass-produced clay drainpipes into significantly deeper drainage trenches than hitherto, usually – as here – at a depth of four feet, or just over one metre. It proved a major breakthrough, and his name soon became celebrated within the farming community. So he was contracted to lay land drains to improve the agriculture of the Great Park.

Just before the track almost coincides with the A332, step onto the grass closer to the road.
Note two lines of veteran oak trees on the far side of the road, stretching into the middle distance. The farther, left hand, one is the western pale of the medieval Great Park. The right hand line is the eastern pale of Moat Park. Near the apparent end of this line one particularly squat stubby oak tree more or less marks the corner where this pale turns westwards (it will cross your path in a few minutes' time). In winter, if you momentarily turn around and look back, you will see veteran oaks on this side of the road, the continuation northwards of the same pale for Moat Park. Sheet Street, as the A332 used to be called, ran between the Great Park and Moat Park pales but was diverted, thus interrupting the integrity of the Moat Park pale.

Continue walking.
About 50 metres from the car park note that you are indeed crossing Moat Park's southern pale, the surviving line of ancient oaks running away to your right, across the side road (Prince Consort's Drive) to Flemish Farm, a little beyond the car park.

Turn right, walk through the car park and through the metal gate on the far side, and pause.
This is Cranbourne, or Cranbourne Walk, a separate enclave within Windsor Forest, formally allotted to the Crown, but only incorporated within the bounds of the Great Park in the early nineteenth century. 'Cranbourne' means either 'heron-stream' or

MOAT PARK AND CRANBOURNE RAILS

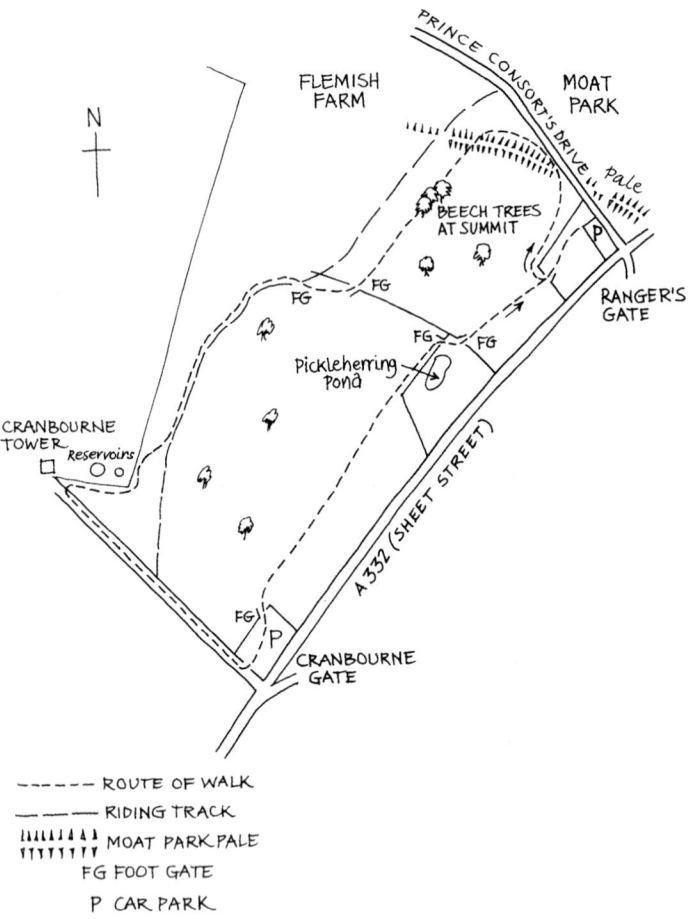

----- ROUTE OF WALK
—— RIDING TRACK
⊥⊥⊥⊥⊥ MOAT PARK PALE
FG FOOT GATE
P CAR PARK

'crooked-stream', depending on whether you take 'cran' to mean a crane or to be the Old English term 'cramb', meaning crooked. At the heart of Cranbourne, at the top of the hill, Cranbourne Rails – we would say 'railings' – was the livestock park within Cranbourne.

If you come across cattle, enjoy them. They are a thoroughly docile delight (see pp. 39, 226)

MOAT PARK AND CRANBOURNE RAILS

Because it is difficult to offer precise route instructions, if you get lost simply enjoy the wonderful landscape. There are a number of gates, as marked on the sketch map, and the A332 is never far away on the downhill side of Cranbourne. You cannot get lost for long, though getting lost is precisely what one should try to do in these Elysian Fields. Once through the gate at the far end of the car park, turn sharp right once through the metal gate and right again, so that you nearly double back. You will see the castle on the skyline. Make for the twin oak trees close to the wooden fence edging Prince Consort's Drive.

Standing by the twin oaks it is apparent that they are on an old bank, indeed the old southern pale, separating Moat Park from Cranbourne, this side of the pale. The pale runs to your right across the road where one can see the ragged line of oaks running back to the A332 and over it. On a map in 1607 the land just inside the Moat Park pale here was marked 'Mother Church', probably a reference to the fact that Moat Park was once held by Walthamstow Abbey.

Turn left along the Moat Park side of the pale, so that you are walking with the wood pasture on your left, and the open field and Prince Consort's Drive on your right. Follow the edge of the wood (the pale follows its edge, overgrown with brambles as well as oak trees) until about 15 metres from the fence ahead of you. Turn left into the wood pasture and wend your way up hill; veer a little to your right in order to reach the summit. You will be joining the track beyond the fence on your right after about 400 metres, so do not stray to your left.

You will know you are at the top, for there are two very old beeches still growing. These beeches were planted about 150 years ago, and judging by their position on top of this hill, almost certainly for visual effect.

Traditionally beech was valued as an energy source, firewood and mast for grazing livestock. By the end of the eighteenth century, however, beech had become fashionable for its beauty as an ornament to the landscape. So beech was planted on high ground to 'complete' a vista. It looks as if this happened here, since beyond are much younger birches which colonised what was open ground. Beech was also popular for furniture, for beech lathes well and so was used for chair legs. You will, of course, be thinking of the Windsor chair industry, which flourished in the nineteenth century. But most of the beech for this came from coppice in the Chilterns. The seats of such chairs were almost invariably made of elm, because its cross-grain can best withstand the pressure of an ample human fundament.

Keeping to the same general direction, with the beeches on your right, follow one of the myriad paths, but at choices veering to your right until you are close to the perimeter fence. Exit onto the track at the first gate you reach. (If you fail to find it, climb over the fence, but if you ever have to climb a fence, please always do it next to a post, and in the case of a gate, always next to the hinge. In both cases this reduces the stress of your weight.)

Turn left up the side of the horse track.
It is here that you face the principal danger on this walk, being charged down by lusty young troopers of the Blues and Royals exercising their mounts. Immediately opposite is a grove of young oaks, perhaps 20 years old.

Very obviously the quality of the woodland has completely changed from what you have just left: here there is an almost complete absence of large oaks and much scrubbier relatively young growth on both sides of the track, indicating that until quite recently, this landscape was open.

As the horse track turns away to the right, watch out for unplanned sycamore growth on your right.

The sycamore is a very vigorous coloniser. It can grow into a magnificent tree, notably in the North and the Borders. In the south-east, however, its reputation is as a pushy uninvited gate-crasher on the landscape. Writing in the late seventeenth century, John Evelyn speaks for many when he deplores it:

> 'The *Sycamor*.... is much more in reputation for its *shade* than it deserves; for the *Hony-dew* leaves, which fall early... turn to a *Mucilage* and noxious *insects*, and putrifie with the first moisture of the season; so as they contaminate and marr our *Walks*; and are therefore by my consent , to be banish'd from all curious *Gardens* and *Avenues*.'

The sycamore has its defenders, as habitat for aphids, thus providing a particularly rich food source for birds. Until recently the tree was almost universally regarded as an exotic, introduced from Central Europe in the Middle Ages. That view is now being reassessed, for there is evidence that the Romans used sycamore extensively in upland Britain. It is now suspected that it may be a native, but that it is happier in a colder climate, hence its stronger presence in Scotland, at and beyond the latitudinal limits of oak.

But why is it growing here? The reason why the sycamore found space to colonise is that the whole of this area lying above the wood pasture was indeed once composed of 'curious *Gardens* and *Avenues*' of Cranborne Lodge, at the heart of Cranborne Rails. By the eighteenth century most of this upper area was laid out with avenues and lawns. When such things are let go, eager miscreants like the sycamore have a field-day. Had the ground here been Bagshot Sands (p. 203), birch trees would have usurped the landscape. As it is, they are only here as a minority.

When you can see it, leave the horse track and make for the wooden paling fence on your right and follow it uphill.
You will notice you cross an avenue of mature lime trees running through the woodland. This is one of several survivors from the ornamental lines and avenues of limes that adorned the hill in the eighteenth century.

Pass the grassy mounds of reservoirs (dug circa 1850) on your right.
The horse chestnuts just before you emerge into the open are recent interlopers, currently under stress from the leaf-miner moth (see p.129). Horse chestnuts were introduced to Britain in the sixteenth century from the fabulous sounding Illyria, today more prosaically known as Albania. They are characteristic of planned parkland rather than countryside.

Face Cranbourne Tower.
This is the heart of Cranbourne Rails, the enclosed livestock park at the heart of the Cranbourne estate. How long there has been a building here must remain open to speculation. One certainly existed in 1486, referred to as 'the new tower or lodge called "the toure in the hethe"'. A lodge was here during the Tudor period. In August 1665 Samuel Pepys visited the house to bring the dispiriting news to George Carteret, Treasurer of the Navy, that the Dutch had destroyed the English fleet off Bergen, Norway. Pepys must himself have been depressed by the bad news he bore, but he also got lost on his way through Cranbourne. Perhaps both factors explain why, while he conceded it to be 'a very noble seat, in a noble forest, with the noblest of prospects towards Windsor',

he also thought it 'a very melancholy place'.

Later, a Lord Ranelagh acquired Cranbourne in 1700 and began spending substantial sums making alterations. The house was magnificent, according to the great traveller, Celia Fiennes,

> 'I drove home by a fine house of Lord Rawnelaughs 14 windows in the front of a square building (much gardening and curious they say, but that Ladyes pride is none must see them) and soe drove a fine gravell road cut with rows of trees: in a mile you come to a broad open way to Windsor....'

If you are wondering where Ranelagh, a man without any large estate, acquired the money for such lavish building, so did Parliament. According to a contemporary, he

> 'originally had no great estate, yet hath spent more money, built more fine houses, and laid out more on house-hold furniture and gardening, than any other nobleman in England. ... Several Parliaments have been calling him to an account, yet he escapes with the punishment only of losing his place...'

Indeed, in 1702 he was caught 'in gross peculation' – massive misappropriation – as Paymaster General of the Forces. He was lucky to escape prosecution, but there is nothing like good connections. Queen Anne, who had just assumed the Crown, was fond of him for his wit and charm.

Ranelagh may have been ousted from his Eden, but he still cared about the landscape he had left. In 1707 he wrote to Lord Godolphin 'praying his lordship's pity for old trees' to protect 'twenty old but beautiful trees', but to no avail. These trees were probably oaks, but possibly elms also. Dismay at the felling of venerable trees has a long pedigree, not least here in Windsor Great Park.

The Duke of Cumberland became ranger of the Great Park in 1746 and keeper of Cranbourne in 1751. On visiting Cranbourne, his father, George II, ordered that 'this and Windsor Great

J. Gendall, East Front of Cranbourne Lodge, c.1823 (photo: EZM).

Park be laid together, for there is but a pail [*sic*] between them'. Cumberland used Cranbourne as a home for part of his stud. It was here in 1764 that a renowned racehorse, Eclipse, was born. Richard Pococke visited Cranbourne on the same day that he saw Moat Park, in August 1754. He was impressed by the siting of the house, 'commanding a view to the west, north, and east as far as the eye can reach, a fine view of Windsor, Harrow-on-the-Hill and Hamsted hill'. Clearly the grounds were still being maintained for 'There is a lawn and walks through the woods about the place.'

The present Cranbourne Tower, built in 1805, is all that remains of the Georgian lodge. The most notable and tragic occupant was the Prince Regent's daughter, Charlotte. Hers is a melancholy tale. In 1814 the seventeen year-old Princess had fallen head over heels for Augustus, black sheep and junior member of the Prussian royal family. This might not have mattered so much had it not been for the state imperative that she should marry William, Prince of Orange, a highly suitable arrangement for the two Protestant states par excellence. It transpired that Charlotte's companion, a Miss Cornelia Knight, had been arranging her illicit assignations with Augustus. When Charlotte broke off the engagement to Prince William, the Prince Regent had her incarcerated in Cranbourne Lodge to cool her heels and her ardour. Since Prinny had comprehensively ignored his daughter until the day she thwarted his plans, no liberal spirit today could possibly take his part even though the wretched Augustus was, by all accounts, a cad and a bounder. Poor Charlotte. Two years later she was married to Leopold of Saxe-Coburg and ten months later died in childbirth. She was only 20 years old.

The lime trees surrounding Cranbourne Tower were probably planted in the eighteenth century, possibly when the Duke of Cumberland was using the Lodge. Look out for the great swags of mistletoe at the tops of the limes, very obvious in winter. Mistletoe enjoyed a reputation of dark mystery for its ability to grow so far above ground and for its ability to remain in leaf when the greenwood was bare, a singularity enjoyed by only two other English native species, the yew and the holly. It became closely identified with fertility, and countrywomen who had difficulty in conceiving sometimes tied a sprig of mistletoe to their waist or wrist. It is propagated by birds wiping their berried-beaks on tree bark. It is extremely rare on oak, preferring soft barks, of which the softest is probably the lime. It also likes apple, on which the berry can be trapped under flakes of bark.

As you look at the tower note the line of limes running down to the left. They are the last ghosts of the principal avenue that approached Cranbourne Lodge in the eighteenth century, very possibly marking the 'fine gravell road' taken by Celia Fiennes.

Turn around and make your way down the tarmac carriageway.
On your left a mass of limes was planted as part of the Lodge gardens.

Continue almost to the A332 and slip into the car park on your left, to re-enter the wood pasture by the foot gate bottom left.
The lower slopes close to the Sheet Street (A332) are essentially wood pasture: open grazed woodland. It is difficult to be sure how old some of the trees actually are. But it is probably these lower slopes of Cranbourne that in 1580, on the orders of Lord Burghley, Elizabeth I's foremost adviser,

> 'had been fenced into the Great Park pales and sown with acorns which is now [1625] become a wood of some thousand of tall young oaks, bearing acorns and giving shelter to cattle, and likely to produce goodly timber as any in the kingdom.'

Supposedly, he established the plantation on account of discovered Spanish plans to burn the Forest of Dean, thus to deny the navy its vital supply of oak. But this must be fanciful, not only because there was plenty of other oak that the English themselves were busily cutting down for housing and for iron foundry furnaces, but because a plot of 13 acres of young oaks could have had no meaningful impact on the size of the navy. More interesting is the rarity of evidence for tree plantations of any size this early. Timber was still normally felled from natural woodland, acorns from the indigenous stock often sown to ensure a future crop on the same ground. Indeed, until the eighteenth century what plantations there were, were usually of oak and intended to become self-perpetuating, like natural woodland. Trees would be felled by experienced woodsmen who knew how to sustain the woodland as well as farm it. All that began to change in the eighteenth century when, devastatingly, the idea of 'improvement' by felling nature's varied and deeply organic woodland took hold. Old established woodlands were often replaced by single species plantations, to be felled in toto on maturity. Furthermore, a growing number of the new plantations were exotic conifer. Beware of people who talk of 'development' or 'improvement'. Too often, the reverse is intended.

As for the cattle, they were certainly not there when Burghley's seedlings were planted (unless fenced in), for they would have made quick work of them. However, 45 years later cattle grazed peacefully beneath oaks large enough to look after themselves. One might have expected the cattle now to be long gone. For a while indeed they were. However, in an inspired move in 2003, five English longhorn cattle were re-introduced to help maintain a landscape of wood pasture. These longhorns, a rare breed now, come from a pedigree herd maintained by Natural England (as English Nature is now known). They are particularly docile, much more so than those dashing young troopers of the Blues and Royals, so have no fear. You will probably get a glimpse of them on this walk and even if you do not, you will be thirsting to know all about them, so there is a note on page 226.

A short way in from the car park was once the site of the goat pen. It was here that the royal goat herd was kept, although in summer months it grazed freely in many parts of the Great Park (for more on goats, and I promise you will not regret it, see p.229).

Make your way through the wood pasture following your own path. It is difficult to get seriously lost (the traffic noise reminds you of your distance from the A332) and there are gates from one section through to another. Eventually one emerges close to the road and the Ranger's Lodge car park.

The delights of this wood pasture need hardly be spelt out. Take your time looking at the ancient oaks here. Each has its own personality. Some are vestiges of their former selves, but where these seem to be but half of what was once there, one will often find a dip in the ground that reveals the enormous girth these trees once had. Except for the noise of aircraft overhead and the A332 on your right, this landscape is about as good as it gets. If you get lost, enjoy it and just repeat the mantra: '*Et in Arcadia sum*'.

Once back at the Ranger's Lodge car park, retrace your way to the car park at Queen Anne's Gate.
You have a choice, either to brave the traffic noise by cleaving close to the road and following Moat Park's eastern pale, or you can follow the track back past Swan Pond, Queen Mary's Plantation and the northern pale to the car park. Either way you will be bordering one side or the other of the Cavalry Exercise Ground. Before the nineteenth century this strip of land was called Long Furlong. In fact it is eight furlongs in length, but the term 'furlong'(literally 'furrow long') has two distinct meanings. It refers to a linear measurement, the optimum length a pair of oxen can happily plough before resting, a point at which to turn the plough. In practice in the Middle Ages this distance could vary enormously, depending on the heaviness of the soil, inclination of the slope and, of course, the strength of the oxen. Technically, however, it became a unit of measurement, 220 yards. Its second meaning refers to an area or square measure, one deriving from usage and clearly the one intended here, the common or open field, or part of it, in which all the furrows lie in the same direction. Unlike Stag Meadow, therefore, this area was under the plough and for a long enough time for it to acquire an agricultural name.

In the nineteenth century it began to be called the Cavalry Exercise Ground, used as such by cavalry regiments stationed in the barracks in Clewer, just north of Moat Park. But it was also used for camps, reviews, polo, agricultural shows and jamborees. In 1957, for instance, 4,000 Girl Guides from all over

MOAT PARK AND CRANBOURNE RAILS   41

Lady Baden-Powell, the Chief Guide, arriving at the World Guide Camp, the Cavalry Exercise Ground, July 1957.

the world camped for a week in the damp grass of Stag Meadow but strutted their stuff on the Cavalry Exercise Ground, where for their grand finale they gathered with another 21,000 Guides from all over Britain around a camp fire to sing the kinds of song Girl Guides like to sing. Among the peerless ditties was this famous song:

Ging Gang Gooly Gooly Gooly Gooly Watcha
Ging Gang Goo Ging Gang Goo *(repeat couplet)*
Haila! Haila Shaila… Haila Shaila Haila whoo *(repeat)*
Shallywally Shallywally Shallywally Shallywally
Umpa Umpa Umpa Umpa *(at which point, the song repeats)*

It certainly makes you think.

WALK 2

Around the Village

FROM RANGER'S GATE VIA SANDPIT GATE TO THE JUBILEE STATUE AND BACK VIA QUEEN ANNE'S RIDE TO THE VILLAGE

Distance 4km: 1½ hours

Warning: In winter months sheep are sometimes grazed near to Ranger's Lodge, in which case walk around the fenced area and pick up the walk again at the carriageway near Forest Lodge.

BEFORE YOU WALK

It is difficult to give this walk a particular theme. It starts by following some of the remaining traces of the medieval park pale, or boundary, of Windsor Great Park, probably created in the mid-fourteenth century. When the pale was erected, it was composed of a substantial bank surmounted with cleft oak palings: together, they constituted a formidable fence over which the deer were unable to leap. (For a short essay on deer parks and pales, see p.192.) Since its disintegration many of the pale banks were probably used as boundary hedgerows. Most of the banks have been completely erased, but in some places we are left with the pale's 'ghost': a slight ripple on the landscape with a few ancient oaks growing out it.

Although they have been marked on the sketch maps, please do not waste time getting frustrated because you are told you are crossing, or are close to, a pale, but you simply cannot see it. It will only spoil your enjoyment of the walk.

This walk returns via the early eighteenth century Queen Anne's Ride to the Village, created in the mid-twentieth century to

AROUND THE VILLAGE 43

accommodate some of the staff of the estate.

Start: leave your transport at the Ranger's Gate Car Park.

(If this car park is full you could start at **Cranbourne Gate car park**, in which case enter the park at the Cranbourne Gate entrance and look out after 200m for the oak on the right of the

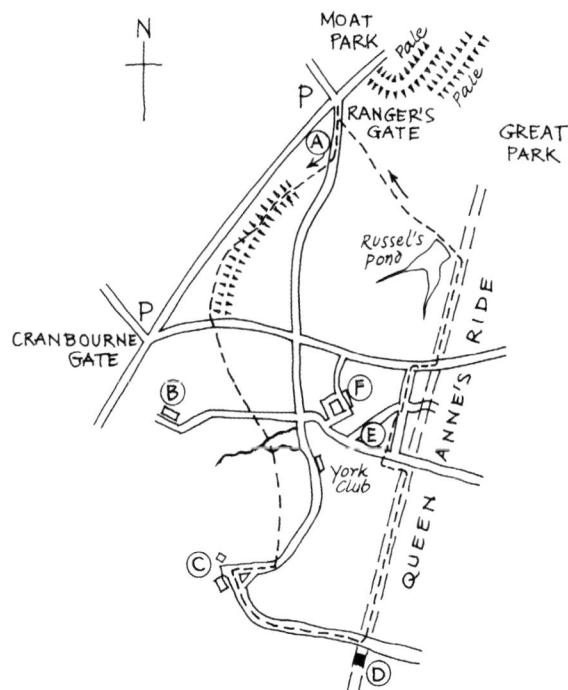

Ⓐ RANGER'S LODGE
Ⓑ FOREST LODGE
Ⓒ SANDPIT LODGE
Ⓓ JUBILEE STATUE
Ⓔ THE VILLAGE
Ⓕ CROWN ESTATE OFFICE & PRINCE CONSORT'S WORKSHOPS

carriageway with a plaque marking Edward VII's coronation in 1902, then pick up the walk overleaf at ➲ (p.45), turning right off the road. It is worth casting an eye over these initial directions before you start your walk.)

Enter by Ranger's Gate and begin by following the tarmac carriageway.
On your right stands the Ranger's Lodge.

Although there were buildings previously on this site, the present building largely dates from 1837, with twentieth century enlargement and modifications. It has acquired a very 1930s look.

Once past the Lodge, after about 150m, make a mental note of the large brick building on the skyline but turn right, off the tarmac, to where the Lodge enclosure suddenly curves away to the right. Follow the line of three oak trees (the last being still young) running out from the enclosure fence.
Looking at the ground between the second and youngest tree, the 'ripple' of the old pale is very clear. The broad sweep of land forwards and to your left was marked on Norden's map of 1607 as 'The Pleck', a word which once meant 'a small trifle' but apparently came to be used simply to denote a piece of land of unspecified size. So we are no clearer what the name might have meant here.

The large brick building on the skyline is Forest Lodge. (In summer its view may be obstructed by trees in leaf.) Start walking towards it, but keep on the left of the line of oak trees straight ahead of you which lead in that general direction. As you approach the third of these trees you should see the 'ripple' of the pale, slightly veering to the left across your path. Follow its direction.

Forest Lodge, once called Holly Grove Lodge, was originally designed by Thomas Sandby, c.1780, on land at that time outside the Great Park, something that will hardly surprise you since you are walking along the course of the old pale. Sandby designed a small four-storey house with classical features. Unfortunately it required heavy renovation in the 1830s and again almost exactly a century later, so that it is no longer recognisably Sandby's work. Sandby worked for George II and was also Cumberland's principal assistant in the Great Park. He played a major part in the restoration and enlargement of Virginia Water. He was a highly regarded neo-classicist. Modest and unpretentious, he instructed that his funeral should be 'without the pageantry of an hearse'. His obituary described him as 'one of the gentlest and best of human beings'. Just thought you would like to know.

Follow the direction of the pale until you reach the tarmac carriageway.
◐ (You will know you are on the right lines as there is an oak with a plaque marking Edward VII's coronation, about 15 paces to your right.) Cross the carriageway, keeping to the same direction. Make for the wooden fence in the distance.
The pale here has been virtually ploughed out of existence except for where a couple of old oaks grow on some rough ground, roughly two thirds of the way to the fence.

Press on to the fence, turn left and follow along the tarmac until you can dogleg right along the fence, even when it eventually seems to descend into a gully. Cross the hidden wooden footbridge.
The footbridge crosses the Isle of Wight Pond. The origin of the name is a mystery. It featured on Norden's map of 1607 at a time when there was no pond, so it may have been a portion of land

caught between marshy ground where streams of the Battle Bourne ran eastwards across the northern part of Windsor Great Park from the higher ground of Cranbourne. But that is speculation. The pond was created c.1800, possibly a belated part of Nathaniel Kent's agricultural improvement (see p. 220). As for the name 'Battle Bourne', bourne of course means stream, but Battle is a modern spelling: of the name Batayle, the family which by 1300 possessed the Winkfield part of the Forest in return for collecting its revenues on behalf of the Crown. In due course the district acquired the name Batayle (or Battle) Bailiwick. This area, a couple of miles west of the Great Park, is the source of the Battle Bourne.

Once on *terra firma*, maintain the same direction with the fence on your right.
On your right, on the far side of the field stand two or three large oaks. They are growing out of the old pale. On your left you may notice you are walking through a plantation of oak trees. Each represents a Commonwealth country, planted to mark the Queen's coronation in 1953.

Through these trees you will see on your left a long brick building. It is York Club, the staff community centre. It is the brainchild of Eric Savill (see p.139), who kept an eye open for valuable items going a-begging. After the 1939-45 War, he asked Vickers-Armstrong if, rather than simply demolishing the steel frame of an aircraft factory it had established on Smith's Lawn, near the Flying Barn (see p. 98), he could be given it, and it was duly re-erected here. With voluntary evening help from park staff and partly donated materials, the present building was established as a staff clubhouse. It was on opening the York Club in July 1951, that George VI announced that the Woodland Garden (see p.143) created by Savill should be known as 'the Savill Garden'.

Keep walking until the path veers right taking you onto to a tarmac carriageway. You will be following the left fork of the carriageway, but before doing so, go up to the gate into the Sandpit Gate complex.

As you approach the buildings you will soon realise from the barking that the Park kennels are located on the right. These must be about the finest dog kennels imaginable, beautifully built during the First World War, palatial accommodation for the royal shooting dogs.

The name, Sandpit Gate, goes back to the late fourteenth century if not earlier, indicating sand extraction was already well-established here. It lies on the old line of the medieval park pale.

It was here also that George IV kept a menagerie, a fashionable accessory to a great estate in those days. His mother, Charlotte, had kept a menagerie at Kew, right beside her *cottage ornée* at the south end of the Gardens. George built up an astonishing and wide-ranging collection, which included kangaroos, cockatoos, emus, parakeets, ostriches, kangaroos, quaggas (south African relatives of the ass and the zebra), a llama and a giraffe. The giraffe died after a couple of years. George took Princess Victoria

'George IV taking his favourite exercise near Sandpit Gate', *Melville, 1830.*

to see his menagerie in 1826, when she can only have been seven years old, but in later life she recalled seeing 'wapitis, gazelles, chamois etc'. On his accession William IV closed it, wisely sending the animals to the new London Zoo.

About 50 metres on the left of the gate stands the pink-hued lodge, designed by James Wyatt shortly after 1800, and still looking essentially the same. A guidebook dated 1827 notes, 'its pleasing appearance is much heightened by the ivy with which it is mantled in several places'. But, as any buildings inspector knows, ivy is extremely destructive of mortar and render, and so it was removed. Wyatt, the uncle of Jeffry Wyatville (see p.112), had established his reputation as a Neo-classicist, but in later life he turned to the Gothic style. Inspired by Strawberry Hill, a lighthearted and amateur confection, Wyatt made a serious study of Gothic and can claim to be the father of the Gothic Revival. His most significant surviving works are Ashridge (Herts) and Belvoir Castle (Leics). Wyatt was a chaotic businessman, taking on far too much work, failing to keep his accounts in order and frequently failing to keep his appointments. So he drove many clients witless, but fortunately 'he had such a peculiar talent in making everyone feel that he was so entirely absorbed in the wishes of his employer that his want of respect in not coming was soon forgotten.' He reckoned he drove about 4,000 miles yearly in his work, rigging out his carriage as an office so as not to waste time. In 1813, aged 67, he was being driven in his carriage at great speed near Marlborough when it overturned, killing him instantly. It was typical of Wyatt that he died intestate and penniless.

Return 20m to the fork and now turn right along the tarmac (southwards).

Watch out for the view over the fence on your right, one of three where you will be rewarded with a great sweep of open country to the south. The wide avenue of young trees is the southernmost end of Queen Anne's Ride. Looking out on this delight, it is difficult not to believe that all is well with the world. At the end of the walk crossing the A332 to return to the car park will remind you of the harsher reality of a profoundly imperfect world.

Follow the road to the Jubilee Statue.

This extremely competent equestrian statue of Elizabeth II, by the sculptor Philip Jackson, marks her jubilee as sovereign in 2002. It tells us of her hippic passion but not of that quality that affects us all, her unswerving sense of duty. Judging by its likeness, it may have been inspired by the 1977 Silver Jubilee oil portrait by Susan Crawford.

Queen Anne's Ride was laid out in 1708 by Henry Wise, one of England's great gardeners of the day. Queen Anne was addicted to the chase. She liked to get to the action fast, hence her enthusiasm for a network of avenues across the park, but her crippling rheumatism and growing corpulence compelled her to hunt by carriage, hence these avenues were known as 'chaise-ridings'. Jonathan Swift saw her here in the park in July 1711. It was a formidable sight and, as Dean of St Patrick's Cathedral, Dublin, he instinctively described the sight of her in biblical terms: 'she hunts in a chaise with one horse and drives furiously like Jehu and is a mighty hunter like Nimrod'.

Admire the lime trees surrounding the statue, predating it by almost exactly 300 years, particularly those on the rear (south) slope. They mark a climax in Queen Anne's Ride, before it sweeps

AROUND THE VILLAGE

Henry Wise, An Accurate Plan of Windsor 2 Parks & Part of the Forrest, c.1712, showing an overview of the Great Park. Note that south is at the top of the map. Queen Anne's Ride slices through the landscape, meeting the ride from the Great (Cumberland) Lodge towards Sunninghill Park, and providing quick access to the area of Windsor Forest most favoured at that time for hunting.

on southwards to Leiper Hill. They are worth admiring since the common lime (*Tilia* x *europaea* L.) seldom reaches this age. The fashion for lime avenues had taken root in England in the 1630s, due to French gardening influence. Even if these trees were reared in an English nursery, they are probably of stock imported from France or the Netherlands, which supplied enormous quantities to England during the seventeenth century for the creation of avenues on great estates. Wise may well have reared these lime trees himself at Brompton Nursery, where he worked in partnership with another great gardener, George London.

Looking southwards, one can see the extension to the Ride, running across open country in another compelling idealised vista.

Turn around and start walking down Queen Anne's Ride towards the castle.

In the distance Windsor Castle scarcely requires comment in its romantic far-off mystique, enhanced in hot weather as it shimmers in the haze. You will notice that the avenue is composed of young trees, planted in 1992 in a major exercise to revive the avenue. Felling old trees is usually a difficult decision. Old trees are host to a myriad of life forms that do not exist in young trees. Fell the lot, and one can destroy an important ecology. Fell only a few and you end up with an avenue looking moth-eaten. Here the presence of many veteran trees close to the avenue ensures other hosts for many invertebrates. But the felling and replanting would not have occurred without very careful assessment beforehand of the impact. Today the avenue, with immature trees, cannot look its best but after 30 years it will look wonderful and promises to be good for at least the next 200.

After 300m, the York Club will soon come into view on your left, across the greensward.

When you reach the tarmac carriageway, turn left and right after a few paces onto the Village Green – but before turning right, walk a few yards on to just beyond the Green and enjoy the delights of the Village Post Office and General Stores, where you can seek welcome refreshment.

Beyond the Post Office, hidden by trees lie the Prince Consort Workshops, built in the 1850s, and also the Crown Estate Offices.

(The Prince Consort's Workshops are not within the area of public access, but deserve a brief note. They were constructed in the 1850s and 60s, and named after the Prince Consort after his death in 1861, though he had never himself been involved in the project. The intention was to provide workshops, top-lit sawmills and accommodation for the Great Park's workforce, both labourers and livestock. The architect was Samuel Sanders Teulon, who usually specialised in an idiosyncratic and high Victorian style. Part of the complex was burnt down in 1906. A new block on the north side of the yard now accommodates the Crown Estate Offices, designed by Rodney, son of Sydney Tatchell (see below), in the 1960s in the vernacular style.)

Refreshed, return to the Green.

Planned villages exist in England but are the exception rather than the rule, unlike Scotland where such villages occur through much of the country. This one was designed and laid out during the 1940s, incorporating six dwellings from the period 1905-08, but with the addition of 32 in the years 1948-49. These houses are deeply in the English vernacular tradition. The Village comes close to, but somehow skilfully avoids, being twee. The regimented spacing between the houses is offset by the variety of architecture as you walk across the green. The Village exudes an air of quiet rural prosperity. Somehow we know we are in rich productive countryside. It almost seems like a life-sized version of the Beaconsfield model village, and we half expect Miss Marple to emerge from one of the houses, basket in hand. But this is a stage-set that works. The credit must go to Sydney Tatchell, the architect, who seems to have been inspired by the architecture that sprang out of the Arts and Crafts movement and was taken forward by those who planned such locations as Hampstead Garden Suburb, New Earlswick (York) and Letchworth: Raymond Unwin, Barry Parker and Patrick Geddes, visionaries who built as they did because they also believed passionately in social justice. Tatchell probably knew these luminaries, since he had designed many town and country houses in the early years of the century and by 1930 was a leading figure at the Royal Institute of British Architects. Across the Green marches a row of oaks, the ghost of an old hedgerow, a nice reminder of the continuity of human endeavour on this ground.

Turn right on emerging at the very bottom of the Village and resume walking down Queen Anne's Ride.

Behind you, you will see the enormous millstone, set on its side. It was quarried in Derbyshire in 1825, but never apparently used. It was brought here in 1992 to mark the re-planting of Queen Anne's Ride.

After 500 metres, turn half left down the horse track across the bottom of Russel's Pond.

The pond dates from c.1700. Russel, however, seems to have been a farmer here in the early nineteenth century.

Follow the track up Beehive Hill, back to Ranger's Gate.

As you come over the crest of the hill Ranger's Lodge lies before you. As you emerge from the trees on either side of the track, look out for an oak on your left standing a few yards beyond the other trees. In winter and spring you will notice the ripple on which it stands. Look through the gate on your right and you will see an apparent avenue of veteran oaks in the middle distance. The line of trees on the right mark the Great Park pale continuing northwards. The lines of trees on the left (which you may notice turns left) belongs to the pale of Moat Park, probably of about the same vintage. Sheet Street, alas now the A332, used to run between the two pales, until it was diverted away from Ranger's Lodge, c.1800.

If you started at Cranbourne Gate, when you reach Ranger's Lodge, turn left to follow the initial walk directions to complete your circuit.

Around the perimeter of Norfolk Farm

WALK 3

Distance 8km: 2½ hours

BEFORE YOU WALK

Norfolk Farm itself is private, but this walk takes you clockwise from Blacknest Gate approximately around the farm perimeter. Norfolk Farm acquired its name in the 1790s, at the same time as Flemish farm, when the farming expert Nathaniel Kent (see p. 220) was commissioned to review and improve farming techniques here. He introduced the 'Norfolk four-year rotation' of crops, hence the new name for the farm. This rotation: (i) barley; (ii) clover; (iii) wheat; (iv) turnips, obviated the need to let the land lie fallow each third or fourth year. This rotation had been evolved by 'Turnip' Townshend (see p. 223). Norfolk Farm remains committed to methods that conserve the environment.

From the South Car Park on the A329, turn left towards Blacknest Gate.

A gate lodge was first built here in the 1760s, but the pink turreted lodge you now see is largely the result of the extensive repairs carried out by Jeffry Wyatville in 1834 after the original building had fallen into delapidation. The castellated turrets and gothic balustrades around the roof are characteristic of Wyatville's desire to camp up the romantic potential of any building he could lay his hands on. He was already the flavour at Windsor Castle, where he 'improved' on the efforts of previous builders to make the look of the buildings less stark and more picturesque (see p.112).

3 AROUND THE PERIMETER OF NORFOLK FARM

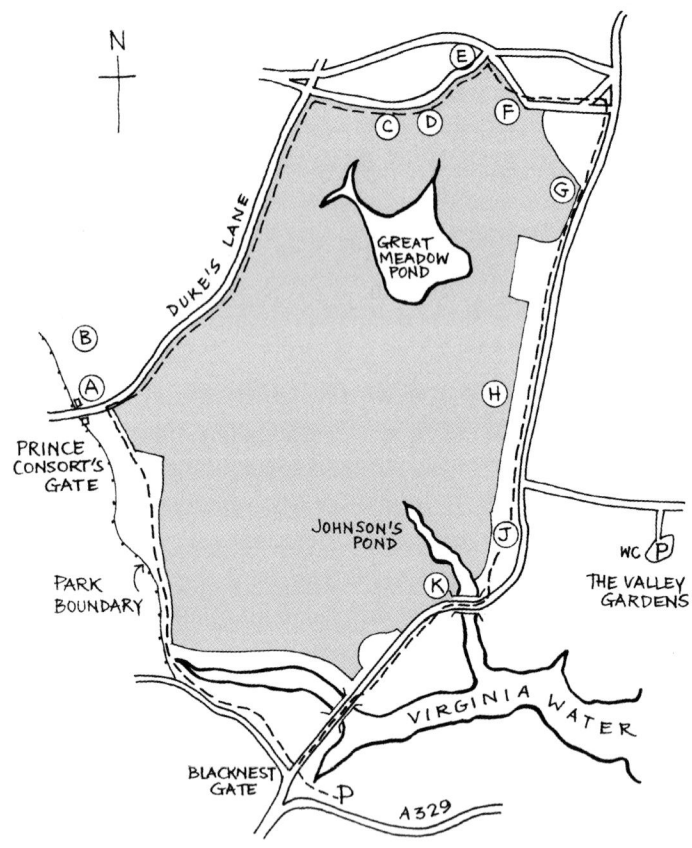

CLOSED AREA

- Ⓐ PARK PALE TRACES
- Ⓑ LEIPER POND
- Ⓒ MEZEL COTTAGES
- Ⓓ THE ROYAL SCHOOL
- Ⓔ CHAPLAIN'S LODGE
- Ⓕ CUMBERLAND LODGE
- Ⓖ CUMBERLAND GATE
- Ⓗ PRINCE CONSORT'S STATUE
- Ⓙ HYDRANGEA GARDEN
- Ⓚ HIGH BRIDGE

Cross the road to follow the horse track for almost 2km until you reach a tarmac carriageway (Duke's Lane).

This first section is through woodland, and there is very little to say. Almost immediately on your right you will pass a Norwegian spruce plantation, and beyond it a few immature monkey puzzle trees (see p.76).

As you walk look out for muntjac deer, most easily seen in the winter months when cover is minimal. You will probably see their telltale cloven hoof prints on the horsetrack. Muntjacs have a hunched appearance in flight, head down and tail raised to reveal white hindquarters. They were introduced from east Asia to Britain in the late nineteenth century and, having escaped captivity, gone feral. Muntjac are reckoned the oldest of all species of deer, extant for about 20 million years. *Homo erectus* has been around for up to 1.8 million years but we, *Homo sapiens sapiens*, for barely 100,000 years or so, so we are very much newcomers on the scene. These creatures may be imported exotics, but their prehistoric remains have been found in France and Germany. The scientific name for the species is *Muntiacus reevesi*, after John Reeves (1774-1856), who was orphaned as a boy but educated at Christ's Hospital and able to find work with a tea broker. In 1808 he joined the East India Company and was posted to Canton as a tea inspector. Before he set sail for the east, however, he had met and been fired up by the great Joseph Banks (see p.159), who urged him to collect botanical and natural history specimens. Reeves made his name with his drawings of flora and fauna, most notably over 300 species of fish, mostly unknown in Europe.

As for the muntjac here, apparently several of this species were released from Whipsnade Zoo in 1921, hence their spread (at least as far as Derbyshire and Wales) and continuing prodigious expansion. Unfortunately, with their voracious appetite they threaten the natural landscape. Their browsing is the chief threat to ancient woodland, far worse than vandal tree felling. By eating out the 'bottom' of woodland they destroy young growth of a whole range of plants, from saplings to ground cover. Thus they deprive birds of nesting cover near the ground, an essential for warblers, nightingales and nightjars. They likewise destroy the ground cover on which small mammals depend, and once these are hunted to extinction their predators, owls, find their food source gone. Dealing with deer is a major conservation problem as yet unsolved.

As you reach the tarmac road (Duke's Lane) look straight across the road. You will see that a track leads to a gate. To its left and parallel to it you will see a ripple of ground. It is the trace here of the medieval pale for the Great Park. (Behind you it runs southwards on the east side of the track you have just walked, but is only discernible seasonally when the bracken has died back.) Six hundred years ago it would have had cleft oak staves forming an impenetrable fence, something of an irony given the ease with which muntjac get about now.

Turn right and walk for 2km along the road.
As you walk along Duke's Lane you will notice that old oaks line this road. The lane was laid by the Duke of Cumberland when he created the Great Meadow Pond. The new pond obstructed one of Queen Anne's avenues, which ran from Bishopsgate on the east side of the Great Park, to the south-west side of the park, not far from here. You may notice that some have magnificent burrs on them, a characteristic of veteran oak trees. These tumour-like and often hairy protuberances arise for a number of reasons, most commonly the chance growth of dormant buds. Burrs are greatly sought after by cabinetmakers for the beauty of their grain.

Keep your eyes open for pheasants and hares in these fields.

The 'old English' pheasant, without a white collar, is not a native but was introduced from the Caspian region before the Norman Conquest. Today you are more likely to see the Chinese ring-necked pheasant, which is otherwise very similar to the 'old English' variety. It was introduced in 1785 and, having been bred for sport, is now widespread as a wild bird, but the two breeds have greatly hybridised.

Hares are an elusive and more precious sight in Britain today. During the twentieth century they are reckoned to have declined to one quarter of their number in 1900. Yet they can occasionally be spotted here. They are the most mystical and magical beast of the field. The hare, not the bunny rabbit, was the true pre-Christian symbol of Easter: a potent symbol of spring, regeneration and new life. A late thirteenth century English poem gives the hare many names, among them 'the way-beater', 'the hedge-frisker', 'the stag-of-the-stubble', 'the light-foot', 'the sitter-still', 'the one that does not go straight home'. So if you see one, do not take it for granted. You have been privileged to see one of the great sights of English nature.

You will pass a turning on your right leading to Norfolk Farm. This is more or less the spot where the Queen transfers from a petrol-driven carriage to an open horse-drawn one, on her way to Royal Ascot each year.

Farmland already existed here when George III commissioned Nathaniel Kent to improve the potential in the Great Park in 1791 (see p. 220). His findings were not encouraging:

> 'Most of the deep loomy parts covered with Rushes or Mole Hills and the upper or higher parts with Fern or Moss… The Farming System was… bad as the Arable was scattered over all parts in some places in single Fields… nor was it under any regular course of cropping or Stocked with suitable cattle…

3 AROUND THE PERIMETER OF NORFOLK FARM

Norfolk Farm, as first proposed by Nathaniel Kent in 1791, situated on the west side of Duke's Lane. It is likely that the farm buildings eventually erected south of the Great Meadow Pond look very like, or identical, to these.

Some good Meadows which is the only valuable part… Being about 150 acres, and three old inclosures of arable land about 50 acres…. All the rest of this Farm consists of Land that turned very little account, the high parts were intirely covered with ling, or weak fern, and the lower parts with long coarse sedgy grass, or the worst sort of goss [gorse].'

Looking around the southern end of the park, Smith's Lawn, the Valley Gardens and the edges of Virginia Water, even the uninformed eye can quickly see how discouraging the prospect is for both livestock and crops. Though better than the Bagshot Sand further east, the terrain is still sandy and acidic. Nevertheless, Kent laid out an ambitious new farm of 1056 acres, tended according to the best agricultural practice at a time when Britain was developing farming skills ahead of almost all Europe, except for the Netherlands. Originally it was intended to incorporate the lands on the west side of Duke's Lane and, indeed, to place the farm buildings on this side, adjacent to the lane. In the event, the idea was abandoned and, unlike the avenue from Bishopsgate, Queen Anne's Ride survived, and the farm buildings were placed south of Great Meadow Pond.

Kent was able to spend only a few days at Windsor each week, so he delegated to the steward, Joseph Frost. He provided

'Norfolk Men' who were skilled in turnip production but as he noted in May 1792:

> 'I am sorry to remark that they have not had the assistance they ought to have had, in excuse for which, Mr Frost alledged [sic] many reasons some of which I was obliged to allow and others I have endeavoured to correct by as much reprehension, as…. it was prudent to give…'

Kent had good reason for his displeasure, for he sensed that his instructions were being deliberately flouted (as you may discover on Walk No. 4, p. 91).

Today the farm is 1,345 acres in size, farmed with a conscious attempt to encourage wildlife. The arable was put to grass in 1880 and the farm buildings demolished with the exception of the original farmhouse and adjacent stabling, which cannot in any case be seen from the road. The farm was revived during the Second World War as a contribution to the war effort. Today it supports Ayrshire, Jersey and Sussex cattle, Wessex Saddleback pigs, oats, beans, barley and wheat.

Notice the wooden fencing on either side of road and one realises what a harmonious effect it creates, delightful where barbed wire is visually jarring. On your left you will pass oak groves, some boasting magnificent 'stag heads', dead branches of oaks that have died back to conserve their energy in old age.

Approaching the crossroads, note the two cottages, Appletree Cottage and The Hollies on your right. There is nothing remarkable in the buildings themselves, but look at the gardens which are in striking contrast to the very English landscape outside. The reason is simple. Almost all the flora is exotic, principally from natives of North America and East Asia. Note the cabbage palm (*Cordyline australis*), a member of the lily family, incredibly including the onion and asparagus. Wonders will never cease. The cabbage palm was first brought to Britain from New Zealand in 1823, so it has been around for a long time.

At the cross roads, half left on the skyline you will see the silhouette of the Village, where many staff live, and half right between the trees (when they are not in leaf) there is a glimpse of the Copper Horse, unnervingly minus its plinth.

Turn right. This is another old road, probably laid during the English Commonwealth, in about 1650.

After about 50 metres, just after the Victorian building (Hollybush Cottages) set back but facing the road, there is a brief glimpse on your right of the Great Meadow Pond, the Duke of Cumberland's first hydraulic essay in the 1740s, before he realised the potential of the valley to the south. He enlarged a much smaller pond, Mistle Pond, which already caught water draining from the west close to Sandpit Gate, before running on through 'Cawseway Ponds' (now Johnson's Pond) southwards to the Virginia Stream. It was only a matter of time before Cumberland asked himself where this water went, and saw the potential of creating a larger lake (which you can circum-ambulate on Walk No. 4.)

Keep walking. After 500 metres pass buildings on your right. After the farm buildings look out for Mezel (corruption of Mistel) Cottages, built in 1936, and bearing the cipher of Edward VIII. These are beautifully designed exteriors, which proclaim the possibly imagined traditional values of rural England. Fantasy or reality, relish the handsome materials, the brickwork and the handmade roof-tiles.

Next, the Royal School, established by Prince Albert in 1845 for the children of estate staff but actually built the following year by John Phipps, the Assistant Surveyor of Works and Buildings. One hundred and fifty years ago, boys and girls were strictly segregated on account of the acute dangers of familiarity with the opposite sex. It is strange how before puberty one fears 'contamination' by the opposite sex and after puberty longs for it. In retrospect one can see what a poor preparation this segregation was for convivial connubial relationships. It was another half century before the husband's right to beat his wife was finally outlawed. Washing, baking and dressmaking were essential parts of the curriculum, but presumably only for girls. Today, one can imagine with envy the delight of being educated here, with so much open space to play in. May it be that today the boys are learning to wash, bake and dress-make too.

On your left at the top of the hill stands the Chaplain's Lodge, an unremarkable house built in 1907.

On reaching the T-junction, take the turning signposted Cumberland Lodge/Royal Collection Store, but almost immediately branch left through the trees and across the greensward, passing the front of Cumberland Lodge until reaching the lime avenue up to the lodge.
(On mistletoe and why it loves lime trees, see p. 37.)

Turn left on the tarmac. At the T-junction 100 metres later turn right. Follow the road past Cumberland Gate.
On your left you pass six semis, see p. 100. Cumberland Gate Lodge (on your right) stands on the Berkshire-Surrey border (see p. 99).

AROUND THE PERIMETER OF NORFOLK FARM

Follow the straight road southwards across Smith's Lawn (if you mind the traffic whizzing past you on the carriageway, slip to your right to the side of the horse track which will take you parallel to, but at a distance from, the dread internal combustion engine). Norfolk Farm once extended across all this land to include the Savill Garden, Obelisk Pond and all the high ground above Virginia Water.

You will be desperate to know the identity of Smith, but you must brace yourself for disappointment, for no one knows for sure. The best bet is that it refers to Thomas Smith, keeper of Manor Lodge (see p.192), after the Restoration in 1660. But the Lawn is popularly associated with Barnard Smith, the Duke of Cumberland's stud groom when the mighty racehorse, Eclipse, was born in 1764, the year of the great eclipse. This, though, is unfounded, for the name 'Smith's Lawn' was already in use by 1748, when Barnard Smith was still too junior to be celebrated in this way.

Smith's Lawn.

What you see across to your left is, of course, highly unnatural. This enormous greensward is anything but native to this landscape. The true landscape, as it was until the end of the eighteenth century, was a forbidding expanse of heather, furze and acid grassland plants. In the 1790s Kent tried to improve the land here, previously used to graze sheep, the classic heathland practice, to render it arable. By 1811 the effort had been abandoned and the terrain reverted to heath again. One must, however, assume that some effort to level the terrain had survived.

With the advent of war in 1914 this area was used for military encampment, presumably prior to embarkation for the Western Front. In January 1917, however, it became the site for a hutted

AROUND THE PERIMETER OF NORFOLK FARM 65

Tented Camp on Smith's Lawn, 1915.

Base Depot for the Canadian Forestry Corps. The CFC had been rapidly formed and the first contingent had arrived in Britain in May 1916, less than four months after London had appealed to Canada for the urgent supply of teams of lumbermen. Until then Britain had been receiving much of its timber from Canada, but it was facing a crisis. The British merchant fleet was inadequate for the munitions, food and other supplies essential for the war effort, but its capacity could be increased by felling trees in Britain rather than tying up part of the fleet shipping timber from Canada. With most British lumbermen enlisted in the armed forces, it made sense to obtain lumber teams from Canada. By July 1916 the Canadians had established a camp at Virginia Water, on the Clockcase Estate (on the A30 at the junction with Christchurch Road). Their sawmill worked 24 hours a day for a year before being overhauled.

The Base Camp here covered no less than 125 acres, composed of the prefab collapsible huts the Canadians were also manufacturing for the war effort, at a rate of 72 huts per

The Canadian Forestry Corps Base Camp, showing the small mill and factory for manufacturing huts, 1918. Flying Barn Cottage can be seen in the distance, Sydney Penhorwood Collection.

When men were men…. The Canadian Forestry Corps felling trees in the Great Park, 1917, Sydney Penhorwood Collection.

month, the component parts loaded onto wagons and taken to Egham station. The Base Camp was also a clearing station for lumbermen despatched to 70 forestry operations across Britain. In the period to April 1918 some 24,000 personnel had passed through Smith's Lawn. Apparently, even the Canadians were astonished by the size of the trees in the Great Park, a matter of some wonder since Canada boasts real giants. However, at the behest of Britain, the Canadians committed arboreal carnage here, felling thousands of great trees.

Later, Smith's Lawn was levelled to be an airstrip where Edward, Prince of Wales, completed his flying training, and where he subsequently often came to fly. In the Second World War it was used by the US Air Force, which kept 14 Dakotas here. It must have become crowded, for after D-Day the RAF had a Tiger Moth training camp here, while Vickers Armstrong also had two aircraft workshops, one of which survives in the guise of the York Club (p. 46).

On your right, after almost one kilometre, you will pass the Prince Consort's Statue. It is a heavy number, a gift to Queen Victoria from the Women of the British Empire in 1887. One's first reaction is that this must have been an unsolicited gift, but apparently not. The Queen had indeed asked for it. But, having asked for it, she did not place it at the end of a vista, for example on Queen Anne's Ride, or closer to the Castle, but thoughtfully tucked it away in this unobtrusive spot.

On your left, the final destiny of Smith's Lawn is unmistakable. It became the home of the Household Brigade polo club, now renamed as the Guards Polo Club. It is open to any polo player wishing to join. In the early days of the Guards Polo Club, in the late 1950s, the crowd of spectators occasionally exceeded 10,000.

Polo is an ancient and deeply addictive game, indeed possibly the oldest game on horseback after the simplicity of competing for whose horse goes fastest, which must be the oldest mounted sport of all. Polo was played in Persia in the pre-Islamic period and its popularity spread. Saladin, twelfth century Saracen champion against the Crusaders in Palestine, was a polo addict. So was Tamerlane, in central Asia in the early fifteenth century. He left behind a polo pitch in Samarkand. Another addict was the great Safavid ruler of Persia, Shah Abbas, 1586-1628. In establishing Isfahan as his capital he laid out a polo pitch in the very centre of his city. It remains an astonishing open space, with the stone goal posts surviving to this day. The Moguls took the game to India, which is where the British fell for it in the mid-nineteenth century. The game was soon adopted by British cavalry regiments, first in India and then in Britain.

If you do not know the rules, here are the basics. The pitch is 300 yards long, with goal posts at each end. The full game has eight chukkas, or phases, each lasting 7 minutes, when a bell is rung and the chukka ends when the ball goes out of play. There is a three-minute interval between each chukka. Because it is so energetic, ponies play only two chukkas in an afternoon, with a rest of at least one chukka in between. Each player is handicapped, according to skill.

It was supposedly a gentlemanly sport from early times. The ninth century Muslim philologist and historian, Abu Hanifa al-Dinawari, thought 'a player should strictly avoid using strong language and should be patient and temperate'. More recently this kind of injunction has taken a few knocks, as the correspondence column of the *Horse and Hound* reveals. In the mid-1950s, for example, that era when politeness was more highly valued than it is today, one polo pony trainer, in disagreement with another, opined that the latter should 'have his head not hacked but sawn off with a blunt saw'.

The truth is that polo engenders passions on an entirely different scale from the priorities of other mortals. It also gives rise to single-mindedness. How else can one explain another letter in the *Horse and Hound*, dated 2 May 1959, commencing with a hint of innocent hurt, 'Sir, – Why is it that there are no facilities in London for businessmen to practice polo?' Even if you do not share his dismayed bewilderment, Saladin, Shah Abbas and Tamerlane would certainly have done.

Polo, as played here, relies on teamwork of a very high standard. It is not to everyone's taste. An RAF officer in Iraq, 1929-30, recalled the delight of playing with local Iraqi police. It is subversive stuff (which may throw light on the travails of that unhappy land):

> 'I laugh a lot during play, and everyone laughs a lot. The laughter is of the simple type, and is nearly always evoked by the misfortunes of one or other of the players… A splendid freedom and sense of individuality prevails. Above all there is none of that depressing element, team spirit, to throw a wet blanket over proceedings. … They do not want their side to get a goal; each one wants to get a goal himself. It is a glorious release from the obligations which beset the team games played among Englishmen…'
>
> A.D MacDonald, *Euphrates Exile*, London 1936.

If you have a sneaking sympathy with that RAF officer, keep your lip firmly buttoned here on Smith's Lawn. If you are lucky enough to see players practising or playing, simply enjoy the spectacle. It is easy to see how one might oneself become intoxicated. However, please think about your bank balance before you get carried away. By 2020, to become a playing member would cost you £22,000, and then there's the annual subscription of £7,475…. So, unless you have just won the Lottery, confine yourself to the visual pleasure.

When you reach the end of the Lawn, slip beside the horse track on your right and follow it down Breakheart Hill, through the back of the Hydrangea Garden.

The Hydrangea Garden

In the nineteenth century botanists recommended planting hydrangeas in 'the yellow loam of Hampstead Heath and some other places'. Well, this is one of those other places, for the 'yellow loam' on Hampstead Heath is in fact the self-same Bagshot Sand of Smith's Lawn and the Valley Gardens. This garden was developed in the mid-1960s to provide late summer interest on the edge of the Valley Gardens, although some hydrangeas will be found inside the Gardens proper. It is composed of drifts of a small number of established cultivars, predominantly blue and white. The principal blue hydrangeas here are *H. macrophylla* 'Générale Vicomtesse de Vibraye', and a darker blue 'Niedersachsen'. The blueness is dependent on the presence of aluminium in the soil. The climbing plant, *H. anomala* ssp. *petiolaris* grows up some of the oaks on this slope. Another white hydrangea here is *H. paniculata*, a tree that can reach 9 metres in height, with great panicles of creamy white flowers, which by September have started to turn pink. Like the *petiolaris*, this plant was collected by Europeans in Japan.

Rejoin the tarmac carriageway to cross the head of Johnson's Pond.

Johnson's Pond formed between 1750 and 1785, and named after

Detail of The Great Bridge over the Virginia River, *by Paul Sandby after Thomas Sandby.*

a keeper living at Manor Lodge (see p. 192). It replaces a series of three ponds down this valley referred to above and known on the Norden map as 'Cawseway Ponds'.

Continue, close to the carriageway, to cross the High (or Five-arched) Bridge.

This bridge was built in 1827. Cumberland commissioned Henry Flitcroft to build a bridge here in 1754. Flitcroft had come from humble beginnings; his father was a labourer at Hampton Court. He owed his advancement to a lucky accident. He fell off a ladder, working on Burlington House and by chance Lord Burlington witnessed the accident and not only paid for medical treatment but took the lad on as an apprentice draughtsman. Flitcroft is now chiefly remembered for the interior decorations of apartments at Woburn Abbey and also for his Temple of Apollo (an imitation of the Temple of Venus at Baalbek) at Stourhead. Here, his design was a single span of 165 feet in oak, 20 feet wide and arching to 20 feet at the centre above the water. It was ingeniously constructed so that, in the words of the diarist, Mrs Delany, 'any piece that is decayed may be taken out and repaired without injuring the rest'. How cunning. Yet not cunning enough for the rigours of Virginia Water and by the 1780s the bridge was derelict and therefore demolished. Mrs Delany had herself crossed the bridge in 1757. She had not dared to drive across, though carriages did indeed cross every day. Even walking across, she thought it 'desperately steep'.

Oak itself is great material for bridge-building. An older bridge, built in 1729 to link Fulham with Putney, lasted until 1880, carrying substantially more traffic. The problem here, however, lay in the design, intended to allow pleasure craft, including a faux Chinese junk to pass under on its way to the China Island. The span was greater than that of the Rialto Bridge in Venice and the stress must have been considerable. When the oak bridge decayed, another bridge, this time in stone, was designed but it lasted even less time. When Jeffry Wyatville was asked to repair the bridge, he said he could build a better one for less than the cost of repairs, and this is what we now have.

Return to the South Car Park.

Virginia Water

WALK 4

Distance 10km: 2½ hours

This walk follows the perimeter path clockwise around Virginia Water, beginning at the South Car Park (A329), but it may be undertaken from any of the surrounding gates, picking up the commentary below at the appropriate point.

BEFORE YOU WALK

You may appreciate a brief history of Virginia Water before setting out. The first mention of a place called Virginia, spelt 'Vergeny', is in an Egham burial record for 1654. Eight years later, in 1662 Virginia appeared, properly spelt, marking a house on a map, just outside the Great Park. The proximity of the *New England Inn*, close to where the *Wheatsheaf* now stands, is probably as much explanation of the name as one will ever get. You would be the poorer, however, not to know of a more enterprising spelling in a record of labour dated 1721, which referred to 'a place called fir Jeny Warter'.

Water has always drained eastwards through the valley from the higher ground on the north, south and most importantly on the west. Indeed, this water created the valley. Yet it remained a stream until the Duke of Cumberland (for his early life, see p. 95) was appointed Ranger of the Great Park in 1746 and began to interest himself in the landscape. In this, of course, he was not alone. By the mid-eighteenth century preoccupation with the landscape, and how to enhance it, had become an obsession with almost everyone possessing a large estate. This passion had been engendered in Britain in the early years of the century by the dramatic fall from fashion of traditional and highly formalised gardens. The new Whig elite began to denounce 'the formal mockery of princely gardens' which was associated, in the minds of supporters of the new constitutional monarchy, with the absolute rulers of continental Europe. By the 1730s the English landscape movement was well under way, pioneered by men such as William Kent who, in the words of his admirer, Horace Walpole, 'leaped the fence and discovered that all nature was a garden'. Cumberland, then, was joining a well-established fashion and doing little more than his parents and his elder brother Frederick had done, at their respective estates running side by side between Richmond and Kew. There, lakes had been dug, 'wildernesses' created, clumps of trees planted and fancy temples full of classical and other cultural references sited among sequestered groves. Finally, the pastoral scene had been completed with the livestock of Arcadia: docile sheep and cattle, duly attended by deferential rustics.

But whereas the landscape between Richmond and Kew, being river meadow, was boringly flat, Cumberland was endowed with a wonderful hilly landscape in which more exciting things could be done. At first he was more preoccupied with creating Great Meadow Pond, which cannot be visited but can just be seen in the distance on Walk No. 3, and also with the planting of avenues and groves in the neighbourhood of his residence, later to be known as Cumberland Lodge. He was the first to lay out plantations here with an irregular outline. Previous plantations had all been square, rectangular or rounded. By 1749 he had begun to look at the southern end of the park with a view to 'improvement', the great landscaping word of the day. That year he made a start with a sluice on the principal stream running into the valley from the west, Mill River, thereby creating a small lake at the far westerly end of the land, the pondhead and sluice being almost exactly where the High Bridge is now.

Cumberland saw the potential for a great lake. Indeed, until the construction of artificial reservoirs, what he created, Virginia Water, was the largest ever man-made lake in Britain. In order to fulfil his goal, he acquired land on Shrubs Hill to the south, outside the boundaries of the Great Park. By the end of 1752 he had created a pondhead a few paces west of where the Leptis Magna ruins now stand, and allowed a lake to back up westwards. He apparently used local labour, 'employing the industrious poor in works of public utility…. about five hundred different people who otherwise must have been greatly distressed'. He used them, too, for the construction of amiable rides and drives and the establishment of ornamental trees. These trees were natives, most notably oak, beech (now depleted and the rest close to their lives' end) and sweet chestnut. In 1754 Gilbert White of Selborne received a letter from a young clergyman extolling the plantings of Virginia Water, 'they are not in ye pretty way in any Part, but in the Princely and magnificent.' Indeed, it was a sight to behold and other visitors came, among them Richard Pococke, who called it the Serpentine River:

> 'This river extends two miles in the park, and farther into the forest; it is made by collecting the waters of the several springs and rivlets round about; at this end it is, I believe, a quarter of a mile broad, and is kept up by a head, which is made into a fine terrace; it goes under a bridge; and forming a little lake, it falls down a cascade made of great stones thirty feet deep, which shows how great a work it was to make a head that keeps up the water in that manner…. On the Serpentine river is a small yatch [*sic*], which has sailed on the sea, a chinese

ship, the middle of which is high, covered and glazed, a
Venetian gondola, and five or six other kinds of boats…'

Cumberland would have adored Disney World. Pococke also noted Cumberland's enhancement of the landscape:

'About fifty yards from the pales on each side of this water, the
Duke has planted large trees, and small ones between them,
with a winding walk thorough, and between this and the
walls is to be a fine lawn, part of which is made and more is
preparing.'

Cumberland's promenades demanded more land, and in 1763 he negotiated the acquisition of a belt of land around Blacknest Gate. He died, still a relatively young man, aged 45 in 1765, probably the unhappy consequence of his progressively expanding *embonpoint*.

Anyway, *après lui, le déluge*, for a torrential late summer downpour in 1768 broke the pondhead he had built and, according to the *Annual Register*, 'several persons were drowned in different places as well as horses, oxen and hogs'. It was George III who reconstructed Virginia Water in the 1780s, enlarging it eastwards to its present dimensions. He took more land into the Great Park in order to ensure not only the dimensions of the new lake but also amiable promenades around it.

From the car park kiosk, walk straight ahead and turn left on reaching the lake. Turn right along the carriageway up to High Bridge (if you wish to read about it now, see p.71), but turn left along the greensward path just before it.

As you walk you will see on your left a plantation of Norwegian spruce and beyond it a curious plantation of monkey puzzle trees. Monkey puzzles (*Araucaria araucana*) are native to Chile and Argentina and belong to the Araucariaceae family of conifers, in nature confined exclusively to the southern hemisphere, probably living fragments of the ancient continent of Gondwana. Forget about monkeys, for these trees predate primates by a good 120 million years and probably evolved their unappetising leaves to deter dinosaurs. The first monkey puzzle was introduced to Britain by the collector and surgeon Archibald Menzies, who brought five seedlings to Kew in 1795.

Menzies had travelled as naturalist and surgeon on the sloop HMS *Discovery* in 1791 under Captain George Vancouver, himself a veteran of Cook's voyage to the south Pacific. When the *Discovery* put in at Valparaiso for urgent repairs, Menzies and Vancouver rode inland to Chile's capital, Santiago. They had been strictly forbidden to explore, for the Spanish were understandably suspicious of Britain's acquisitive intentions. They dined with the governor, a man with the improbable name of Don Ambrosio O'Higgins (father of the more famous Bernardo, a man born out of wedlock but destined to become hero of Chilean independence). It was in his dessert that Menzies struck lucky, for there he espied the seeds of the monkey puzzle. Almost certainly too challenging to swallow whole (the seed can measure up to 4 x 2 cm), he must have pocketed a few, perhaps by coughing into his napkin, unless he took the risk of breaching etiquette by asking Don Ambrosio if he could save a few samples for propagation. We only know of this story because as an old man, Menzies regaled the young Joseph Hooker (see p.179) with the tale of how he brought the first monkey puzzle to Kew. A far greater problem lay in wait for Menzies: propagation of the seeds on board His Majesty's Ship *Discovery*. On the return journey the *Discovery* dropped anchor in the Shannon in September 1795 and it was from here that Menzies wrote to Joseph Banks (see p.159), who had arranged his journey, reporting that Captain Vancouver had held him under arrest since late July. Menzies' instructions to his manservant for nurturing his seedlings under their glazed frames on the quarterdeck had

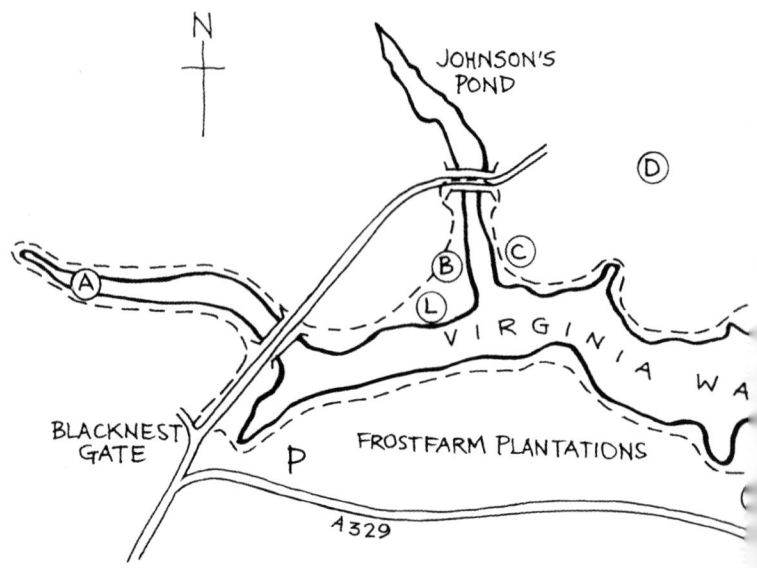

been countermanded by Vancouver. The man had been sent off to help crew the ship. The consequence was that many plants had perished. When Menzies expressed his dismay, Vancouver, mindful of his absolute powers on board his own vessel, had him arrested. There must be more to this tale than meets the eye. One can imagine that the two men may well have got on each other's nerves, spending five years in close confinement together. But there is another mystery. Menzies' journal of the voyage ends very abruptly in February 1794, eighteen months before his safe return to these shores. Did Vancouver remove the later entries, and if so, what did he wish to remain secret? We shall never know.

On your right lies 'the Mill River', Cumberland's first waterworks here. No trace survives of the pondhead and sluice. A little further on, now overgrown and close to silting up, lies 'China Island', the artificial island left in the middle of the Mill

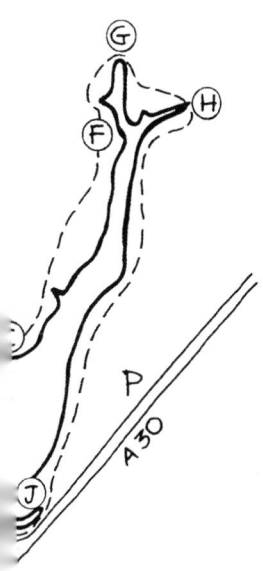

- (A) CHINA ISLAND
- (B) VIRGINIA WATER COTTAGE
- (C) HOLLY GARDEN
- (D) PLUNKET MEMORIAL
- (E) BOTANY BAY POINT
- (F) TOTEM POLE
- (G) ETON BRIDGE
- (H) LARCH BRIDGE
- (J) CASCADE
- (K) LEPTIS MAGNA
- (L) SITE OF:
  (i) The Medieval Manor
  (ii) The Fishing Temple

River. It was here that Cumberland erected an oriental teahouse, a cod-Chinese confection that gave the island its name. Caroline Powys, taught to keep a diary by her father, visited the island in 1766, and recorded:

> 'We went to the Chinese Island, on which is a small house quite in the taste of that nation, the outside of which is white tiles set in red lead, decorated with bells and Chinese ornaments. You approach the building by a Chinese bridge, and in a very hot day, as that was, the whole looked cool and pleasing. The inside consists of two state rooms, a drawing room and a bed-chamber, in miniature each but corresponds with the outside appearance.'

According to a guide book of 1793, 'the middle room is of scarlet-green, richly ornamented with gold; the panels of the doors are of looking glass... and the other room.... is hung with white satin, painted, in which is a settee of the same.' One must

William Delamotte, The building on China Island, *1829-36.*

regret the loss of this building, but such fantasy gazebos were unable to withstand the elements. Kew had many of them, almost all now gone except for the brick-built Pagoda.

Turn right onto the horse track, cross the bridge and turn right where it states 'No entry for horses' back along the northern bank of Mill River.

This is the least frequented part of Virginia Water, yet in some ways it is the loveliest for its sense of seclusion.

Cross the carriageway and proceed along the footpath that skirts the trees, in due course to pass in front of the houses.

On your left is an example of the once relentless heathland that left Daniel Defoe speaking of a 'barrenness, horrid and frightful to look on' and William Cobbett 'as bleak, as barren and as villainous a heath as man ever set his eyes on' (see p. 206).

On your right, you pass staff cottages, true to their vintage,

1949 and 1906 respectively. Behind them, now inaccessible, lie the remains of the moat of Manor Lodge, the original hunting lodge of the park established at least as early as 1240. Most of it was submerged by the creation of Virginia Water. Yet Manor Lodge was a substantial building in the Middle Ages with its own chapel. The kings of the thirteenth and fourteenth centuries probably visited the Manor Lodge as often as the Castle. It underwent extensive rebuilding and repairs over the centuries before its final demise in the 1790s. After its demolition, George IV had fun with his 'Fishing Temple' here (but this can wait, to be more readily appreciated from the far side of Virginia Water).

Keep walking straight with the trees and rhododendrons on your right, towards the bridge.

You may note as you continue to walk towards the bridge across the head of Johnson's Pond that there are traces of earth banks with veteran oak trees. It is impossible to tell precisely what they represent, but there were a number of enclosures attached to Manor Lodge established here over the centuries. These are probably ghosts of the old hedgerows or pales.

Rejoin the carriage at the bridge over Johnson's Pond.

It was here that Wyatville built a wooden 'hermitage' for George IV in 1827, a rustic structure under which the waters of Johnson's Pond cascaded into Virginia Water. It did not outlast the nineteenth century.

It is possible that Fort Belvedere, the erstwhile royal residence on Shrubs Hill, will once more become visible from here, once the vista has been cleared. The view from Fort Belvedere to the Fishing Temple (the site of Manor Lodge) was still clear in the 1930s, but the Temple was demolished in 1936 and the vista lost. Fort Belvedere is famous as the location from which Edward VIII broadcast his message of abdication to the nation, but as Prince of Wales he had already set up his own court here. The Belvedere was originally built for Cumberland in 1753, in a bizarre mix of the classical and gothic styles, but since then much tinkered with. On Johnson's Pond, see p.71.

Cross the bridge and immediately take the path to the right, which cleaves to the lake shore.
After 150 metres you get a good view on your right of Virginia Water Cottage, on the northern side of the moat that once enclosed Manor Lodge. Close by, to the right of the house, is a mid-nineteenth century boathouse, while to the left is the iron trellis bridge, built in 1903, across to the island where Manor Lodge once stood. The Cottage, something of a misnomer given its generous size, was built in the 1870s and was added to in 1904-5. With its lawn running down to the water it proclaims England's Summer, that halcyon period of peace and prosperity that came to an abrupt end in August 1914. It has been a very much more frightening world since then, so relish a moment of illusion.

As you continue, on your left you will pass the Holly Garden. This garden is registered as a National Collection for holly and contains hundreds of cultivars. These are mainly variants on the indigenous species, *Ilex aquifolium*. The wild species here are principally from East Asia and North America.

Holly is one of those plants which have always exerted a strong hold on the imagination. Druids believed that the sun never deserted the holly and thus it was sacred. Our compulsion to bring holly indoors at Christmas is pre-Christian in origin, presumably to do with bringing the sun into our homesteads at the winter solstice. But holly is ambiguous. It was associated with the misrule of Roman Saturnalia, which also occurred in December. Our festive addiction to holly seems to have been continuous. In 1598 John Stow reported how every church, house and street corner in London would be garlanded at Christmas with holly. Pre-Christian Europeans believed it protected livestock. In some Native American tribes, women wore sprigs of holly at childbirth, to ensure a safe delivery. In the wild, here in Britain, the holly manages successfully in the understorey of woodland, overshadowed by oak or ash, and it is there, in the penumbra of woodland rather than as a garden plantation, that it exerts its magic most powerfully.

You will be able to map-read (p.150) which parts of the Valley Gardens you are skirting. Watch out for the few surviving beeches planted by Cumberland as landscaping for his new lake, almost all on the right of the path. One of them bears near the base of the trunk the head and feathered headdress of a First Nation Canadian carved into the trunk. It was the handiwork of one of the Canadian foresters camped on Smith's Lawn during the First World War. For such defacement of a royal tree, one can imagine the tremendous rocket he must have received from his commanding officer, a rocket which may have left him still up there, somewhere in the stratosphere. Back on earth, there are some unusually large and handsome alders along the water's edge.

To your left you will pass the valleys of the Gardens, one by one, with a sweep up the main valley to the Plunket Memorial, a white pavilion in the Palladian style, dedicated to the memory of Lord Plunket, Deputy Master of the Household, built in 1979.

Pause when you reach Botany Bay Point, the open promontory and beach looking across to the ruins of Leptis Magna. I have been unable to establish the origin of the name.

It is intended to re-open the vista to Hangmore Hill, above the Virginia Water car park and beyond the A30 to the south-east.

Virginia Water, drained during the Second World War, revealing the pondhead which had burst in 1768. Leptis Magna can be seen in the background.

It should then be possible to see the Clockcase, a brick tower begun by Cumberland in the style of Strawberry Hill gothic, but only completed after his death. Finished by the 1790s, it was attacked shortly after by vandals who made off with the decorative stonework. By 1819 it was decided to dispose of this white elephant that already required extensive refurbishment. So it was sold by the Treasury for a paltry £1,800. Six years later, however, its inflated value became clear when the Treasury had to pay £8,500 to get it back into Crown hands. George IV had apparently expressed his 'insufferable annoyance' that he and his Court could be observed cavorting at Virginia Water by someone sitting in the Clockcase. Celebrity privacy, one may think, has always been heavily overpriced.

When you reach the Totem Pole (see p.162 if you wish to read about it now), resist the temptation to turn right, and continue to follow the edge of water until you reach Eton Bridge over the feeder stream, cross and follow the path across the greensward, and then turn right to follow the path along the lakeside.

George III, Cumberland's nephew, was the driving force behind enlargement and restoration of the lake, after the first pondhead had burst in 1768. He seems to have thought of enlargement in the early 1780s but it was only at the end of the decade that his ambition was fulfilled. He decided to expand the lake eastwards in order to benefit from water running south from the Cow Pond and the Obelisk Pond. This stream flowed outside the park and therefore the Crown had to acquire part of Egham Wick Farm, now the woodland at the east end of present lake. In order to obtain this land, a private bill was introduced in Parliament becoming an Act in April 1782. This Act referred to the King's desire to restore and extend 'an ancient Piece of Water', something of a whopper, bearing in mind the lake was only thirty years old.

The area after Larch Bridge is a good one in which to look at conifers. When this landscape was planted with trees in the late eighteenth and early nineteenth centuries, exotic and recently collected conifers, principally from North America, were planted here (on conifers, see p.172). They enjoy the poor acidic soil.

As you walk southwards you will note tall waving plumes of purple-headed grass along the fringe of the water. This is common reed (*Phragmites communis*). Traditionally it was used for thatching, but its quality benefits from being regularly cropped. If you wonder why everyone now seems to get Norfolk rushes for re-thatching it is simply because we have short-sightedly drained so much land almost everywhere else. Environmentalists are drawing attention now to the value of wetlands and bogs, not merely as a wildlife habitat but also as a means of water conservation. A newly found function for the common reed is as a filter-bed, purifying polluted water.

Another common water plant around the lakeshore is the bulrush or, more properly, reedmace (*Typha latifolia*), with its characteristic brown bottlebrush head, a plant strangely without any economic purpose in Britain. In Nevada they were used by the Native American communities for boat building.

On your left you will pass the car park and *Wheatsheaf Inn*. The Inn had been mentioned in the Act of 1782. It had been built by John Atkins soon after the original pondhead had been washed away in 1768. Indeed he had been allowed to have this plot 'in exchange for a cottage and piece of Ground situated on a spot now overflowed by Virginia Water'. Atkins' new inn had a very large garden. The Crown was keen to acquire it, since it was uncomfortably close to royal park. If he was to be shifted yet again, Atkins was understandably determined to maximise the compensation. The Treasury was equally understandably dismayed by his determination and it was not until 1826, well into the reign of the privacy-obsessed George IV, that the property was finally acquired, for what at the time seemed a wildly exorbitant sum, £5,000. That sum, in today's money, is roughly £200,000, so one is tempted to conclude that the Treasury got something of a snip. But of course real estate prices were far lower in those days and by contemporary standards the price paid was undoubtedly egregious. As a happy consequence, however, we now enjoy the convenience of both the extensive car park in what was once the garden, and also the conviviality of the inn.

Continue walking due south along the lakeside but stick with the tarmac path to reach the Cascade.

George III's creation of the new pondhead was certainly not trouble free. It was washed away during construction but was finally completed to the king's satisfaction in August 1788, following the reassuring involvement of stalwart chaps from the 23rd Regiment of Foot (subsequently the Royal Welch Fusiliers), encamped nearby in the Forest.

The great sarsen stones were brought here to build the Cascade in 1788. You will be wondering how far they travelled to grace this scene. Remarkably, they are local, from Bagshot Heath. They are the same as the stones used to build Windsor Castle. Yet it was still a nightmare getting them here. In his classic work on the Park, William Menzies set out the oral recollection of a local man, John Tiley, who had died in 1860:

> 'he remembered going when a boy to see this [the Cascade], and that the labourers engaged upon it had great difficulty in finding carriages with axles trees strong enough to carry the large stones used in building the waterfall. Iron, ash, oak, and other materials had been tried but nothing bore the strain so well as green alder newly cut.'

You will also be wondering how the stones were formed. Sarsen stones are very young, made of sheets of Tertiary sands and gravels put down by the great river that flowed over the landscape about 30 million years ago. The combination of water and the silica in the sand re-cemented these sands into extremely hard rock, subsequently broken into blocks by the freeze-thaw action of the Great Ice Age. If you wonder why, when other sandstones are so soft, these are so hard, bear in mind that silica is the same material that makes flint. John Tiley tells us how they were located: 'the labourers used to watch for places [on Bagshot Heath] which turned brown in dry weather, and then bore down upon the stones.' As for their name, 'sarsen', it is an old word for a grey wether (a gelded ram), and one must assume that these grey lumps of stone looked very much like sheep lying down. The walks and rides around the lake were completed by 1790.

William Delamotte, The keeper's Royal *[Virginia]* Lodge, *1828 (Photo: EZM).*

About 150 metres later, you will see a house on the high ground to your left. This is Virginia Lodge. A house was standing here as early as 1746. At this time the house was just within the park and following its refurbishment that year was occupied by the 'Game Keeper at Virginy Gate'. One diarist reported 'The Virginia Water broke [its] head, and is entirely gone, fish and all, and the house in its way carried off as clear as if no house had ever been built there', but it is difficult to imagine it was this house, at such a height above the stream bed. Demolished by floodwater or not, it seems the house was entirely rebuilt during the 1780s, in part to provide visual interest above the Cascade. Subsequently, however, the house had a chequered career, at one point divided into three tenements. It is difficult to recapture the illusion of its original intention, particularly since the 1930s brought it pebbledash and the latest style of window. Only the castellated walls remind one of its former romantic character.

Continue walking to Leptis Magna *(that's quite an instruction).* You may well ask what on earth precious pieces of the great classical city of Leptis Magna are doing here. It was the English consul-general who cajoled the pasha, or more properly the Bey, of Tripoli into gifting these pieces of stonework to the Prince Regent in 1816. Doubtless it helped the Bey reach his generous decision to recall how the Royal Navy dominated the Mediterranean, when necessary with the power of its guns.

Duly despatched, the stones arrived at Spithead in March 1818, and were transported to the courtyard of the British Museum, which must itself have been something of a building site as the present structure was built from 1823-26. It seems no one quite knew what to do with the fruits of this act of vandalism. From 1824 there was some discussion of using the marbles at Virginia Water as scenic ruins but it was two years later, in 1826, that they were finally given this dubious role. Jeffry Wyatville (see p.112), already busy remodelling the buildings of Windsor Castle, was instructed to attend to urgent repair work to the bridge that carried the turnpike road from Wokingham (now the A329), a road which allowed private access beneath for the carriageway to the Belvedere from Windsor Great Park. It seemed the obvious place to deploy the marbles as a classical ruin. Entirely unconnected classical statues off a captured French ship were erected among the columns in a general arrangement to ornament the passage beneath the repaired bridge, and solemnly named 'the Temple of Augustus'. However, visitors to the scene so mutilated the statues that these were removed, in fact to a place of such safety that their whereabouts has remained a mystery ever since. Meanwhile a romantic and garbled amnesia set in regarding the identity and significance of the ruins, so that within the year the ruins were described in a guidebook as 'brought from Greece and the shores of the Levant'. The story then, as myths do, acquired embellishment so that by 1844 a visitor could report, 'I heard from Prince Albert, that all these ruins really came from Athens – had been brought thither by Lord Elgin, and were placed absolutely in very much the same condition as they had been found in their original home.' The only inspired feature here is the cedar of Lebanon.

As for Leptis Magna itself, which of course is worthy of far greater interest, it was one of the great Roman cities of the North African coast from the early second century AD until its demise in the fifth century, the result of creeping sand encroachment and the disintegration of the Roman Empire. It had reached its apogee c.200 AD, under the Emperor Septimius Severus who had himself been born there. The first recorded pillage of its stones was by a French consul in the seventeenth century, who thought Louis XIV would enjoy a small handful of classical columns, allegedly no less than 600 of them, which may have been incorporated into the construction of Versailles and the Tuileries. Despite French and British depredations, Leptis Magna is to this day among the best surviving remains of classical antiquity.

Continue walking.
On your right, on the first headland is where Cumberland's pondhead ran across to the northern shore.

As you walk you will notice large tussocks on the lakeshore. These are greater tussock sedges (*Carex paniculata*). They have probably been planted here but they like fenland and similar wetland. Where they were widespread, they traditionally used to be cut and trimmed to make hassocks (kneelers) for the local church, or used by the poor as fireside seats.

On your left is Frostfarm Plantation, extending all the way back to Blacknest Gate. It was planted with oaks in Cumberland's time, and subsequently with conifers. It derives its name from Joseph Frost, tenant farmer on Shrubs Hill, who was already Park Bailiff, and then General Superintendent under Nathaniel Kent, the newly arrived farm moderniser. In this latter role, Frost proved bolshie, his ego unwilling to accept the authority of his new boss.

In September 1791 Kent had sent Frost off for a week to Norfolk where, he fondly thought, Frost acquired 'a good Opinion of the Norfolk Husbandry'. It was not long, however, before he found that Frost was deliberately obstructing his attempts to improve farm standards. In 1794 he took a starlit walk and found that the sheep had not been folded as instructed, and that his orders were, in fact, being systematically disobeyed. The suspicion must be that Frost was encouraging his subordinates to undermine Kent. Unfortunately we do not know the end of the story, one played out repeatedly in any number of work situations, but it is ironic that Frost – leader of the awkward squad – is immortalised here, while many walkers may never have heard of the enlightened Kent (on him, see p. 220).

Watch out for the inlet of Johnson's Pond on the far side of the lake.

On the left of the inlet stood Manor Lodge, its approximate location marked by the very broad steps down to the water. The lodge was set back behind the present steps. By the eighteenth century the lodge was still bounded on the south and west sides by the old moat, but not on the east side where the moat had already been lost in the outlet for Johnson's Pond. The house by now was what one might describe as plain 'Queen Anne', the popular pre-Palladian style domestic style, but it was a house in

The Fishing Temple, possibly George IV's final version, Virginia Water, *Melville, c.1830.*

slow but inexorable decline. Dilapidation led to its demolition, probably in 1792.

It is from this vantage point that one can best imagine the Fishing Temple, for it stood at the very water's edge on the same site. George IV was an avid angler. In 1825 the Treasury was notified 'a small Fishing Temple should be erected for his Majesty's convenience.... we are informed that His Majesty frequently enjoys the recreation of Fishing upon Virginia Water'. Wyatville seems to have been the architect, and he embarked, no doubt on his master's bidding, on a departure from *faux*-gothic into Chinoiserie. Like so many edifices, this one was amended during the course of construction and, even more predictably, its costs wildly outran the estimate.

Until the Temple was completed, George used tents captured from Tipu Sultan of Mysore during the first campaign against him, in 1791-2. George's mother, Queen Charlotte, had previously used these tents at Frogmore. Once the Temple was completed these colourful items were used as supplementary accommodation for guests. They seem to have been well made since they were still going strong in the mid-nineteenth century. Queen Victoria even used a few of these tents 'at the Breakfasts at Buckingham Palace in '68-69'.

The Temple would have been completed by 1827, except for the fact that George could not resist fiddling with his confection. Specialists in Chinoiserie were brought in, to tart up both the interior and exterior, and to add pavilions for the service staff. The roof was raised, and oriental towers added. The whole was rigged out in reds, blues, greens and plenty of yellow and gilt. It is with first hand knowledge of Brighton Pavilion (and if you have never been inside it, you have never lived) that one can both imagine the utter frivolity of George's imagination and also bitterly regret that the Fishing Temple has not survived for us to enjoy today. Its loss must be placed on the debit side of the sum total of human happiness.

George's Temple was barely completed before his demise in 1830. But the Temple's own well-being depended entirely on the attentive affections of its creator and once bereft of them, it went into rapid decline. For the Temple was a high-maintenance building and by 1833 serious deterioration was reported 'from want of paint', and several carved ornaments were removed. The roof was re-painted but in a plain colour, almost literally one might say, the Writing on the Wall. Prince Albert achieved a stay of the demolition proposed in 1840, but it was finally razed in 1867. By then the Royal Family were greatly distracted by their contrasting summer acquisitions of Osborne on the Isle of Wight in 1845 and Balmoral on the edge of Cairngorm, leased in 1848, and then by the death of Albert himself in 1861.

Nevertheless, a new Fishing Temple did indeed replace the old one, but where Prinny's had been frivolous and therefore irresponsibly delightful, Victoria's was earnest and therefore, judging by its looks, somewhat lowering of the human spirit. The new Temple was in the style of a Swiss mountain chalet, almost as improbable as George's Chinoiserie, but its exterior walls were clad in Staffordshire tiles, patriotically red, white and blue. The architect, Anthony Salvin, was the son of an army general. His principal skill was with regard to his knowledge of medieval and Tudor buildings and so he was a natural choice for the restoration and improvement of castles but hardly for imaginatively conceived fishing temples.

Queen Victoria used the new Fishing Temple only occasionally and it really came into its own for tea parties and shooting in season during the short reign of Edward VII. It was his grandson, Edward VIII, who apparently had it demolished in 1936 because it spoiled his view from Fort Belvedere. But perhaps it was less the building *per se*, than the memories it evoked, of a childhood with a bullying nanny and remote parents.

Keep walking for one kilometre to return to the South Car Park.

Royal Windsor: Cumberland Lodge, the Copper Horse and Royal Lodge

WALK 5

Distance 7½km: 2½ hours

This walk takes you from the Savill Gardens car park around the Obelisk Pond to Cumberland Lodge, thence to the Copper Horse and then back around the Royal Lodge. It seeks to revive awareness of some of the designed landscape which is currently lost, but may be revived.

Start facing the front of the Savill Building Visitors' Centre. Turn left and start walking southwards along the tarmac path. Make for the Obelisk.

The Obelisk stands on Hurst Hill, a place name featuring on Norden's 1607 map, a *hyrst* in Old English being a wooded hill. The Obelisk was established, c.1747, by George II to honour 'the services of his son William, Duke of Cumberland' in his victory over the exhausted and half-starved Jacobite clansmen at Culloden in April 1746. The outcome of the battle was a foregone conclusion before it commenced. Only a murderous decimation could ensue, which it did. Cumberland was only 25 years old at the time, perhaps too young to understand the moral quality of what he was doing. News of his ruthless victory travelled fast and he acquired the epithet 'the Butcher' 500 miles away in London within four weeks. Cumberland inaugurated a suppression of the Highlands, in his own words 'to pursue and hunt out these vermin amongst their lurking holes' and was indiscriminate

5 CUMBERLAND AND ROYAL LODGES

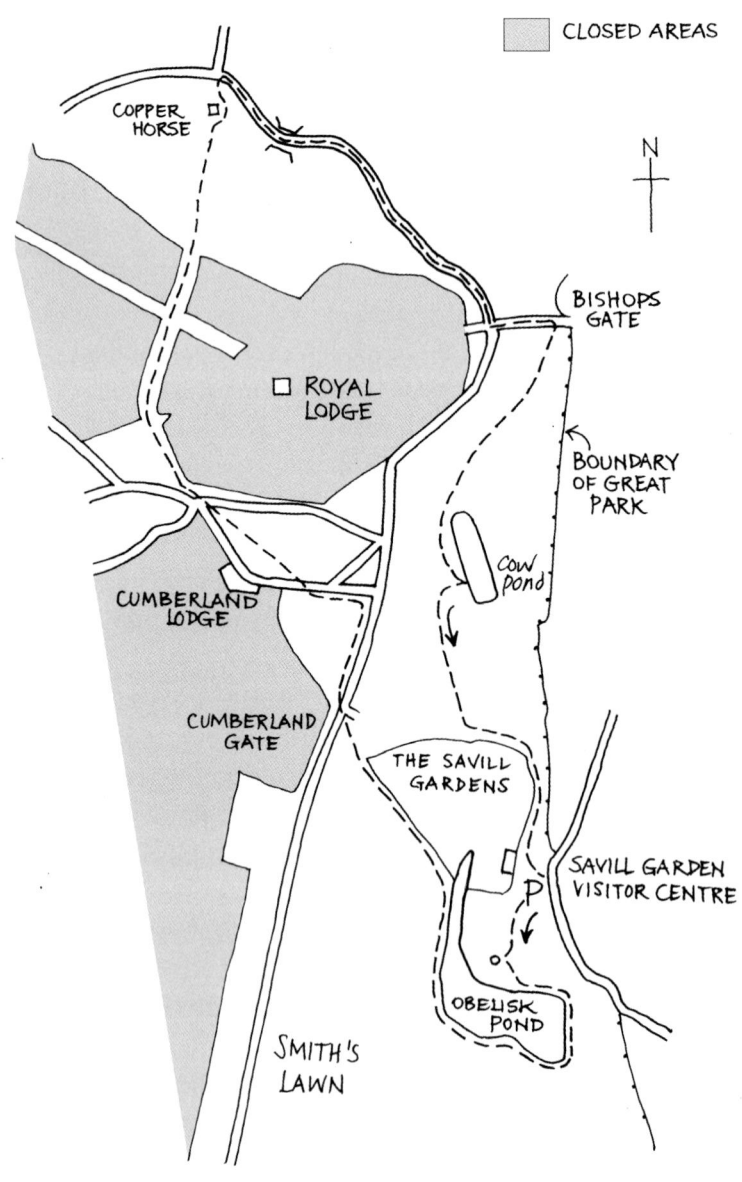

concerning those who had come out for the Young Pretender and those who had not. Handel's 'The Conquering Hero' was first performed in honour of Cumberland, before it found its future place in his oratorio, *Judas Maccabeus*. Today, however, Cumberland would be viewed not as a hero, but as a war criminal.

Here, Cumberland is depicted on top of the obelisk as a sun, its rays shining out. The inscription was only added in the reign of William IV. On the north side of the Obelisk (facing the Visitors' Centre) the word 'Culloden' was inscribed. Queen Victoria, it is said, distressed by what it implied in Highland Scotland, had the name erased and 'Cumberland' carved in its place, hence the otherwise incomprehensibly deep inset of the latter. It confirms her consistent view of 'that dreadful Butcher Duke who she is sorry to think was her Gt-Gt Uncle'. George II intended the obelisk not only as an honour to his second and favourite son, but as a focal point for an avenue of trees running south from Cumberland Lodge, an avenue scheduled for restoration in 2009-10.

Continue walking down the tarmac carriageway.
You will notice to left and right some magnificent conifers, including cedars (of Lebanon and the Deodar, see p.174) and also the giant sequoia or 'Wellingtonia' (see p.173). On your right lies the Obelisk Pond, created between 1749-50 by Cumberland during his major landscape work here.

Walk around the foot of the pond, crossing the pond head, but once across turn right to follow the path back along the other side of Obelisk Pond.
(You may wonder what lies ahead on the road. It leads up to Smith's Lawn, via the cottage known as 'the Flying Barn'. The

'The Moveable [or Flying] Barn', W. Pearce, A General View…., used to protect the hay while being constructed into a rick, erected in 1792 as part of Kent's agricultural improvements. It was demolished in 1845. The present house is dated 1876.

'Moving Barn' or 'Wheel Barn', as it was also called, is no more since it was demolished in 1845 and the present house does not merit a detour.)

You will find yourself walking about ¾ km through Alder Cover, as it is called, although it is predominantly birch and oak, with only a few alders along the pond bank.

The Obelisk Pond Bridge was built specifically to carry the avenue from Cumberland Lodge to Hurst Hill across the newly created pond. The pond had been created by Cumberland, with the construction of the pond head in 1750. Here, at the tail end of the pond, Henry Flitcroft was commissioned to construct a bridge. Flitcroft designed a bridge to look at, rather than cross. Although built in either stone or brick, with a floodgate, the single arch was steeply sloped and ultimately unsatisfactory, except as an object to look at, which was his primary intention. At any rate, like his other ill-fated structure (see p.71), it was not destined to last, despite repairs in 1783. In 1833-34 Jeffry Wyatville built a new bridge. Unusually for the period, the bricklayers used English rather than Flemish bond. (The difference is that in English bond, alternating courses of bricks have either the sides ('stretchers') or ends ('headers') exposed, whereas with Flemish bond each individual course alternates exposed headers and stretchers.) The other important feature of this bridge is the floodgate within its span, retaining some control over water levels.

When you reach the head of the pond, pick up the carriageway carried by the Obelisk Pond Bridge, turning to your left.
On your right lies the boundary fence of the Savill Garden. A few veteran oak trees survive along this fence, presumably part of the oak avenue planted in 1675 (see below). On your left lies Smith's Lawn.

As you reach a small tarmac track leading into the rear of the Savill Garden, look out for the first house on your right, with a grey slate roof. This is Garden House, deceptively similar to the Ranger's Lodge (p. 44) because it is a modern replica. It was built for Eric Savill (see p.139) following his retirement from Ranger's Lodge in 1959, so that he could enjoy the outlook over Smith's Lawn and stroll through the nearby gardens which he had created.

Turn left along the tarmac track, then turn right, passing Cumberland Gate Lodge on your left.
This south-facing house was originally designed by the now little known Edward Blore. What stands now was built in the 1860s but remains close to his original design. Blore's achievements in the period 1820-50 were very extensive. Among his works were the rebuilding of Lambeth Palace in 1829-38 and completion of Buckingham Palace after the dismissal of John Nash, 1831. He also carried out work inside Windsor Castle. Such a list may seem prosaic, but his ability as an architect to complete tasks within budget was anything but prosaic and remains a quality still remarkable for its scarcity.

5 CUMBERLAND AND ROYAL LODGES

A few paces on, on your right, stand Roundwood, and 1 and 2 Cumberland Gate, examples of the English vernacular tradition.

After 200 metres, pass on your right a group of six semis, in an open rectangle lay-out, set back from the road.
These were built in the years, 1948-54, and are also in the same vernacular tradition. On the opposite side of the road is a stand of sweet chestnuts, planted c.1820. Sweet chestnuts were planted both for their ornamental value and also often for their food value for the deer herd (though these now lie outside the deer enclosure).

Turn left at the first tarmac intersection and approach Cumberland Lodge.
You are now on an avenue, one of several laid out at the end of the seventeenth century to radiate from Cumberland Lodge and marked on the map made by Henry Wise in 1712. This avenue leads from the Cow Pond to Cumberland Lodge. Some of the

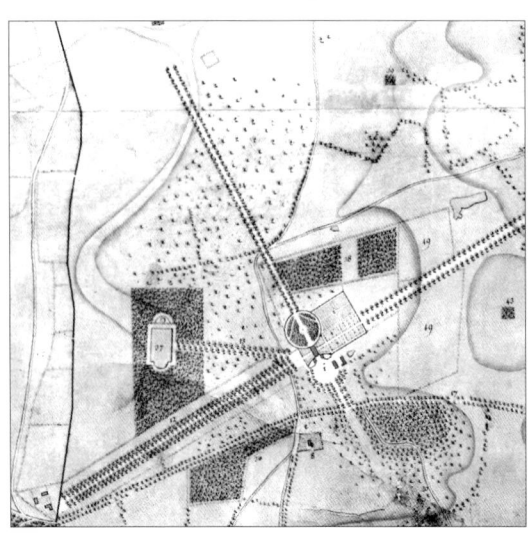

Detail of Henry Wise, A Generall Plann of Windsor Great Park, *c.1712, showing the layout of avenues radiating from the Great (Cumberland) Lodge to Bishopsgate, the Cow Pond, Hurst Hill and across the south of the Great Park. South is at the top. (Photo: EZM)*

original limes trees, remarkably, seem to have survived. One visitor, writing to the Ranger, William Bentinck, Lord Portland, wrote in 1697: 'I have been twice to view your Lordship's garden in Windsor Park, and had great satisfaction to see the very fine avenue to the Lodge so well ordered and in so good a forwardness.' The principal reason they were 'forward' is that in all probability they were brought in great baskets as well-established saplings from the nursery, very possibly the Brompton nursery in Fulham. Portland had laid out his garden in the Dutch style, hardly surprising since he had accompanied his Prince, William of Orange, to England in 1688.

At the entrance to Cumberland Lodge you may like to have a thumbnail history. Its origins are republican, for the first house here was built by a Cromwellian cavalry officer, John Byfield, in c.1649. He had made astute use of a situation in which Parliament was strapped for cash to pay the army and had adopted a debenture scheme involving the sale of the king's houses, goods and lands. In one contemporary estimate:

> "He did erect one very faire dwelling-house with stables, barns and outhouses answerable thereto, planted orchards and enclosed ye same and garden plots with brick walls and built other farme houses for tenants.'

Restoration year, 1660, put a dampener on Byfield's plans and he was compelled to abandon his enterprise in 1664 when the 700 acres he had acquired and on which he had built his new seat, were returned to the Crown.

The first avenue to the Great Lodge, as the house became known, was a double avenue of oak trees from Bishopsgate, planted in 1675. Another avenue was planted across Smith's Lawn and by the time the Duchess of Marlborough became Ranger in 1702 all the principal avenues had probably already been laid out. That dauntless traveller Celia Fiennes described passing the

5 CUMBERLAND AND ROYAL LODGES

The Great [Cumberland] Lodge, c.1754, after Thomas Sandby.

house on her right as she rode northwards towards Windsor:

> 'you come to a broad open way to Windsor [Sheet Street/A332] on the left hand, on the right to a little house of the Dutchess off Marlboroughs which is very exact gardens and fountains cut hedges and groves pailed in, from this house is the fine gravel walke continued very broad between high rows of trees on one hand a fine grove of straite trees.'

The Duke of Cumberland became Ranger in 1746 and immediately modernised the gardens, converting the formality of the Queen Anne period to idealised parkland. Among other things, a double row of beeches was planted inside the double row of oak trees leading to Bishopsgate (to be exact 90 metres south of the present gate) planted seven decades years earlier. It was incontestably the finest avenue of the period in the park, just under 200 metres wide, and bordered on either side by a hedgerow. It was presumably originally intended to move the gate to meet the avenue. Sadly, except for the occasional isolated tree, no evidence remains of the Bishopsgate avenue.

Major fire at Cumberland Lodge in 1869 left the interior almost completely gutted, as *The Times* reported:

'Shortly after 9 o'clock this morning, a fire broke out in the apartments occupied by Mrs Thuroson, housekeeper… An alarm was at once raised… without a moment's delay, messengers were sent by his Lordship [Bridport] to the Windsor Infantry and Cavalry Barracks, when detachments from both barracks, with their engines, were promptly despatched… Unfortunately the nearest supply of water was at Ox-pond [which you will pass later], a quarter of a mile distance… At half-past 11 o'clock the roof fell in with a tremendous crash…'

Much of the building was gutted. Although the books were rescued from the library, the pictures were engulfed in flames in the hall, to which they had been taken for safety, before they could be removed.

Cumberland Lodge underwent extensive refurbishment again in 1911. In 1947 it became a study centre, the outcome of the vision and energy of Amy Buller, a university teacher shocked by the ease with which Nazi ideology was able to take hold of a European society. She very much wanted to form a 'college of Christian philosophy' but had no premises in which to establish it. In 1944, someone had put Buller's book, *Darkness over Germany*, into Queen Elizabeth's hands. It was not long before Buller was invited to the palace for a conversation. One thing led to another, and in 1947 Amy Buller found herself (the way one does) in conversation about her project with George VI at the Royal Lodge. Looking out of the window towards Cumberland Lodge, the king said: 'Now I think that's the house you ought to have for your experiment… I think it might suit very well.' Thus, the Lodge became the venue where students and teachers could come, in her own words, to:

'examine the fundamental assumptions underlying the springs of political or economic or scientific action; and in so doing be given an opportunity of examining the Christian philosophy of life in relation to all this.'

Although a Christian foundation, it has never had a proselytising purpose. More to the point, it represents the quintessence of the liberal society, arranging conferences, retreats, seminars and public conversations, all directly or indirectly aiming at the betterment of society. How 'woolly cardigan' you might think, but in reality we cannot have enough of liberal values at the beginning of this already deeply troubled new century.

Having faced the Lodge, turn right and walk between the Lodge hedgerow and the tennis court, and maintaining the same rough direction cross the open grassland (you should pick up a rough track) to reach the crossroads at the Chaplain's Lodge. With the Chaplain's Lodge entrance more or less straight ahead of you, take the sandy track forking right, which leads downhill, with the wooden paling fence of Royal Lodge on your right.

You are descending into 'Deep Strood', clearly marked on Norden's map of 1607. You will be grateful that it no longer lives up to its name, for a 'strood' (Old English) was marshy ground overgrown with brushwood. On your left in the trees you will pass Ox Pond, doubtless one good reason why the strood has ceased to be. It is unclear how old the pond is, but it was certainly here by 1750.

You will come to a wide grass lane between hedgerows leading to the Copper Horse. After 250 metres, pause at the junction of grassy tracks.

To your right you will see the rear of Royal Lodge, and one of the vernacular staff houses of the estate. The tree line is dominated

How the south front of Royal Lodge looked in George IV's day, The King's Cottage, Melville, 1830.

by exotics among which the Cedar of Lebanon is predominant, an immediate indicator of the grounds of a great house. What you see now is very largely the work of George VI's rebuilding during the 1930s, which effectively destroyed all but the Dining Room of George IV's creation.

This is almost the best view you will obtain of the Royal Lodge (there is a better view up the slope if you remember to look back as you approach the Copper Horse), and you will probably be wondering why it is so deeply secluded. The reason lies to a large extent with George IV. As Prince Regent, George intended using the lodge as temporary accommodation while Cumberland Lodge was being refurbished.

The house had already passed through many hands. A dwelling was first recorded here in 1662, occupied by one of those who benefited from the Parliamentarian victory over the Crown in the Civil War. In the early eighteenth century it was called the Garden House, apparently on account of the garden produce its grounds provided for the Great [Cumberland] Lodge. By 1750 it was known as the Dairy, but this is far too modest a description for a house containing a dining room and parlours on the ground floor, and several bedrooms upstairs.

So it is hardly surprising that in the last years of the century it became known as Deputy Ranger's Lodge. By 1800 it had been enlarged with a two-storey wing, and the entrance dignified with a pedimented and columned porch. It was about this time that the house was occupied by Joseph Frost, the Park Bailiff and General Superintendent, the man who had gone out of his way to undermine Nathaniel Kent (see p. 91). Frost had been there a decade when it was sniffily noted, 'Mr Frost resides in the Deputy Ranger's Lodge, a Residence much beyond his rank and situation…[and] would be more properly inhabited by some Gentleman, whose service the Prince Regent could constantly command.' In fact, enter Prinny himself.

The house may have been too grand for the likes of Joseph Frost, but to Prince George, moving in in 1813, this gentlemanly residence was a delightful 'Cottage'. With the refurbishment of Cumberland Lodge now predicted to take much longer than anticipated, enlargement of the Cottage was inevitable and John Nash, who was to acquire far greater fame with the Pavilion in Brighton and urban development up to and including Regent's Park in London, prepared additions which enlarged the house at least threefold, including a conservatory measuring 75 by 40 feet. Prinny never did anything by halves and he soon inhabited the largest cottage in Christendom.

Prinny knew perfectly well that he was unpopular, mainly for his dissolute life but also for his treatment of his estranged wife, Caroline. Knowing himself to be unpopular he secluded himself. The more he secluded himself the more unpopular he became. He hated members of the public trying to get a view of him, so he tried to banish unwanted people from the park, and would even check that 'the coast was clear' before driving around the Great Park in his phaeton. He grew plenty of leaf cover around his lodge and also diverted some of the principal routes through the park away from his residence.

Things came to a head in 1820 when, on learning that her father-in-law was dead, Caroline returned to Britain to claim her rightful place as consort of the new King. She rapidly became the focus of support for all those who were critical of George. Few cared for Caroline, who had herself been pretty wayward, except as an instrument against an unpopular new king. As a ditty of the day succinctly put it:

Most Gracious Queen, we thee implore

To go away and sin no more;

But, if that effort be too great,

Go away at any rate.

Alas, she did not oblige. When, at his coronation the following year, the great doors of Westminster Abbey were slammed in her face, her bid for the consort's throne collapsed and by then her cheerleaders had vanished and she returned home amidst the crowd's jeers. A week later she was dead. But George was joyously free. Improbably, people forgot his dissolute past in the splendour of his coronation, for which Parliament had set aside well over £9 million in today's money. He even dared visit Edinburgh in 1822, the first Hanoverian sovereign to do so, and it was a wild success, skilfully choreographed by Walter Scott, an extravaganza of tartanry that from that time became the sartorial statement of a whole nation.

To continue the story, you must reach the Royal Lodge gatehouses facing Bishopsgate.

Continue up the lane to the Copper Horse.

Perhaps the first thing to know about the Copper Horse is that it is not made of copper, but bronze. There are 25 tons of melted down brass cannon in the finished article. The sculpture, of George III, is the work of Richard Westmacott, who was commissioned by George IV in 1824. The reason for its immense size is to ensure it is properly visible from the Castle. For this, Westmacott was definitely the right man.

You will have seen Westmacott's work before, for he it was who produced the statue of *Achilles* (1814-22) at Hyde Park Corner, to celebrate Wellington and his achievements. Westmacott revived large-scale bronze casting in Britain and liked to refer to Greco-Roman art. In the case of *Achilles*, he drew upon *The Horse Tamers* in the Quirinale, Rome. *Achilles* proved controversial, for this huge male nude was funded by modest British gentlewomen to celebrate a general no longer, by any stretch of the imagination, in his physical prime. Once cast at Westmacott's foundry in Pimlico, a committee met before the statue's erection to contemplate it. After considerable deliberation and excitable correspondence it was decided that public taste demanded a fig leaf be duly affixed to the offending organ. Nevertheless, the press had a field day, dubbing the monument, 'The Ladies' Fancy Man'. It did not help that the sword was put into *Achilles*' hand only after a considerable delay, so he looked more prize-fighter than warrior-hero.

Here, Westmacott was inspired by the statue of Marcus Aurelius on the Capitoline Hill. Yet where Marcus Aurelius and his mount were mean and hungry, Westmacott depicted George III as he indeed was, well-fed and distinctly portly, and that demanded a chunkier charger to bear his considerable weight, hence all that tonnage of brass. It took time to produce and was still at the Pimlico foundry when George IV expired in

1830. Moving the sculpture to Windsor was a nightmare, the carrier refusing to take responsibility, even though it was still in pieces for assembly on site. Indeed, one horse leg had to be recast because of damage sustained in transit. Meanwhile, Jeffry Wyatville's last commission from George IV was to produce the plinth, which was made of brickwork internally but faced with granite. The sculpture finally arrived here and was elevated in October 1831. According to a local guidebook:

> 'upon its arriving at its place of destination, sixteen persons …. got inside the horse, where they partook of a luncheon of bread and cheese, and concluded their repast by drinking the health of William IV, and singing "God Save the King".'

At today's prices the statue had cost a little over £1 million in all, approximately two-thirds on the sculpture and one third on the plinth.

Inscribed upon the plinth are the words, 'Georgio Tertio Patri Optimo Georgius Rex'. There is much more to this than meets the eye. George III had hardly been the 'best of fathers' to his son, as the inscription claimed. Their soured relationship was a blot on the political landscape for the last 30 years of George III's reign, and one can only conclude that this statue was an act of filial contrition and motivated by guilt. Things had started well between father and son, for the former appointed not one but two rockers for the royal cradle. Who else gets such a start in life? Yet George III was himself a prisoner of maxims with which we cannot identify today. He insisted that if young George or his brother Frederick displayed any laziness or untruthfulness, they were to be severely beaten. One of their sisters recalled seeing them 'held by their tutors to be flogged like dogs with a long whip'. It hardly bears thinking about. Inevitably in such circumstances the son could not satisfy his father and lived in a permanent penumbra of paternal disapproval.

CUMBERLAND AND ROYAL LODGES

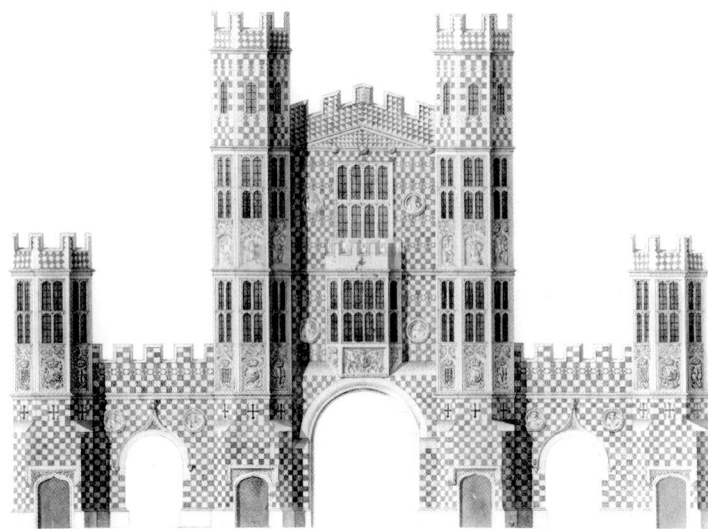

The Old Gate, Whitehall, with additions, as intended as the focal point at the south end of the Long Walk, Thos. Sandby, c.1760. (Photo: EZM)

Subconsciously, young George knew how to punish his father for such cruelty. He acquired a love of dissipation, as he himself admitted. He became 'rather too fond of wine and women'. Prince George's dissolute life has entered our national mythology. In fact his life was profoundly tragic, denied the paternal trust or filial responsibility that might have helped him grow into maturity. As one acute bishop observed, 'he was a man occupied by trifles, because he had no opportunity of displaying his talents in the conduct of great concerns'. When his long-lived father was finally unable to carry on, Prince George was sworn in as regent in 1811. By then he was 49 but completely unmanned by over 30 years' denial of any responsibility. Having become a national joke, he was nationally disliked, his unpopularity reaching a climax in 1819 when he gave his retrospective formal approval to the action of the Manchester magistrates that had led to the Peterloo massacre. Despite all these negative attributes, it is worth calling to mind Prinny's principal virtue. No other British sovereign made such a signal contribution to the arts by his shrewd patronage of fine artists, sculptors and architects.

As for the Copper Horse, it became immediately known as such. Some years later, when Queen Victoria enquired of a guest how he had spent the afternoon, she received the incautious response that he had walked to the Copper Horse and back. Her retort was tight-lipped: 'You mean the equestrian statue of our Grandfather.'

The view. The Long Walk, planted by Charles II, is a statement of power and majesty, perhaps even of '*L'Etat, c'est moi*', true to the time it was laid out, when Louis XIV was creating Versailles, with majestic avenues created by Le Nôtre. George IV had not been the first to think of a suitable completing feature at the southern end of this avenue. The Duke of Cumberland had himself toyed with a visual focus and thought to re-erect the Tudor-period Holbein Gate, which had stood in Whitehall but had been demolished in 1759. Although a magnificent gateway, it might have looked ridiculously out of place isolated in the middle of parkland. We

Harvesting crops beside the Long Walk, c.1945.

are probably much better off with the Copper Horse.

Compare the formality of the Long Walk with the pastoral scene on either side of the Walk, veteran trees growing on a grassy landscape – the summation of England's pleasant pastures green. But do not be deceived. These pastures, 500 acres in all, were only returned to their present state in 1979, after possibly over a century of service as cereal fields. The decision to revert to pasture was taken in the light of the Crown Lands Act of 1961, which stated: 'it shall be the duty of the [Crown Estate] Commissioners in exercise their powers of management in relation to the Windsor Estate to aim at maintaining its present character as a Royal park and forest.' What you see, therefore, is certainly not nearly as 'timeless' as you might be lulled into thinking. But a reversion to the qualities of the ancient landscape was clearly the right decision.

Most of what one can now see of the distant castle is the work of Jeffry Wyatville (1766-1840). His principal patron had been the duke of Devonshire, for whom he carried out extensive work at Chatsworth and to whom he seemed: 'a delightful man, good, simple like a child, eager, patient, easy to deal with...' Wyatville seems to have had an idiosyncratic mode of speech, a cross between Staffordshire and cockney. He had been commissioned to carry out improvements here in 1824, both to make the castle more comfortable as a residence and to alter the exterior since 'it does not abound in the picturesque parts', as Wyatville himself put it. The picturesque was all the rage.

At the time he was still known as Wyatt, a name that irked because it associated him with his famous uncle, James (see p. 48), and indeed another successful architect uncle, Samuel. Thus it was, that when George IV laid the foundation stone of the new works at the castle in December 1824, Wyatt plucked up his courage to seek the royal consent to add 'ville' to his surname to distinguish himself from his Wyatt kin. George, it is reported, responded characteristically: 'Veal or mutton, call yourself what you like. Its all one to me.'

It is the picturesque that you now see. Wyatville raised the height of the Round Tower and added to the external fabric towers, bays, crenellations and also machicolations, that unsavoury device over gateways used in earlier centuries for pouring molten pitch on particularly unwelcome visitors. (Turn to p.132 for an illustration of how the castle looked in the early eighteenth century.) Today, such reworking of the exterior of an ancient monument would cause national apoplexy. At the time, however, Wyatville was widely admired, not least by his royal masters, for he was duly buried in St George's Chapel.

Facing the Castle, turn right and make your way down to the tarmac carriageway and cross the Stone Bridge.
The Stone Bridge was built in 1829, on the instruction of George IV. It was part of his re-routing of roads, first started in 1813, to ensure the privacy of the Royal Lodge, past which the old road from Bishopsgate to Sandpit Gate had run.

Continue walking.
Watch out after 500 metres or so for an avenue of mature beech trees on your right, once one of the approach avenues to the Royal Lodge.

Pass out of the deer enclosure and pause at the Bishopsgate entrance to Royal Lodge.
By 1824 any pretence that George IV's residence in the Great Park was remotely like a cottage, even a *cottage ornée*, was

abandoned and the present name of 'Royal Lodge' was given to it. It was here, in 1826, as her biographer, Christopher Hibbert, relates, that the seven-year old Princess Victoria was driven over from Cumberland Lodge, where she was staying with her Aunt Gloucester, to meet her sovereign at the Royal Lodge. 'Give me your little paw,' he said, pulling her up onto his substantial knee so she could kiss him. 'He was large and gouty, but with a wonderful dignity and charm of manner.' Much later she recalled it as 'too disgusting, because his face was covered with grease-paint'. At the time, however, she seems like other children to have fallen under the spell of his 'wonderful dignity and charm of manner'. Next day, out walking with her mother, the King came along in his phaeton. 'Pop her in!' he cried, and popped she was, 'greatly pleased' at being given a ride.

Invited over one evening to listen to 'Uncle King's' band playing in the conservatory, in Hibbert's words:

> 'He asked her what tune she would like the band to play next. With precocious tact, she immediately replied "God save the King!" "Tell me," he asked her later, "what you enjoyed most of your visit?" "The drive with you," she said.'

What a pert young madam, you might think, and you would be right. When contemplating the august majesty of the Queen-Empress, it is refreshing to learn that the young Victoria was no stranger to temper tantrums, obstinacy or intemperate behaviour. 'She drives me at times into real desperation,' her distracted mother admitted, 'Today the little mouse.... was so unmanageable that I nearly cried.'

Victoria was no wit, but her uncle most certainly was. On 9 January 1828 the Duke of Wellington waited upon the king at the Royal Lodge. As the Duke recalled:

> 'The first words he said to me were, "Arthur, the cabinet is defunct"; and then he began to describe the manner in which

the late Ministers had taken leave of him on giving their resignations. This was accompanied by the most ludicrous mimicry of the voice and manner of each individual, so strikingly like that it was impossible to refrain from fits of laughter.'

Whereupon, the king invited Wellington to form a new administration.

King George died in June 1830, and this spelt death also to his creation. Within eight weeks a local newspaper had announced 'a great portion of the Cottage is to be pulled down'. Visiting the castle a year later, Charles Greville, the diarist, exclaimed

'What a *changement de scène*. No longer George the 4th, capricious, luxurious and misanthropic, liking nothing but the society of listeners and flatterers… but a plain, vulgar, hospitable gentleman, opening his doors to all the world.'

But this vulgar, hospitable gentleman, William IV, spared the enormous Conservatory and also the recently completed and magnificent dining room at the Royal Lodge. Indeed, he and his consort, Adelaide, visited the remains of the Royal Lodge and occasionally picnicked there. It was still, in the 1840s, in the words of a foreign visitor, 'a sort of compound of summer-house, tent, and richly-adorned country house'. Still quintessential Prinny, in fact.

Over the years various court dignitaries used the building, but by the twentieth century it was becoming seriously dilapidated. In 1931 George V invited his second son, Albert, Duke of York to make something of it as a family home, and this the future King George VI proceeded to do. The enormous conservatory was demolished and replaced with a family wing, and only the Wyatville Dining Room survived the re-construction.

The present entrance drive was only laid out in 1936. The gate lodge and cottages are neo-Georgian, rebuilt in 1949, but they are

CUMBERLAND AND ROYAL LODGES

The original gates, lodges and cottages at Royal Lodge, as designed by Raymond Erith. Photos: A.R. Bowling.

not the original intention. Half of one block of cottages, designed by Raymond Erith, received a direct hit a mere fortnight after their completion in November, 1940. The rest was damaged but not destroyed. Only a repair job was necessary. However, Sydney Tatchell, who was already working on the Village, was invited to re-work Erith's designs. Where Tatchell's cottages have porches with pediments, windows framed by architraves and the whole finished in pink plaster, Erith's were bare brickwork, Suffolk Whites, with slate roofs, very simple, very chaste. Tatchell even replaced the plain iron railings with a stone balustrade. Lucy Archer, Erith's biographer, comments:

> 'Tatchell's changes to these buildings.... were doubly distressing to Erith for not only was there now, as he wryly put it, no trace of his art but his buildings had been given the

very neo-Georgian image he most disliked and against which he had reacted so strongly.'

Only Erith's iron gates survived unaltered.

Turn around and make your way towards Bishopsgate, but watch out for the riding track on your right, and turn onto the footpath beside it.

This footpath avoids the irritation of passing traffic, but more or less shadows the road leading southwards from Royal Lodge. It takes you along the edge of the more densely wooded area to your left. For much of your way there is a stream on your left.

Cross the second small footbridge over the stream, and continue to follow the path.

On your right now you should notice a plantation of oak trees, each with a label at its base. These oaks commemorate the imperial possessions of George VI at his coronation in 1937. The oak, or *Quercus*, genus is very large, with a huge number of varieties. They are laid out in a pattern from north to south, according to the latitude of each possession. The first oak you come to on this path stands for Cyprus, now unsurprisingly dead and shorn of its limbs, iconic for the catastrophe that overtook the island in 1974, with a Greek nationalist coup followed by the Turkish invasion. Perhaps it will come to life again when Cyprus is reunited. Palestine comes next, a surprisingly healthy *Q.conferta*, perhaps a symbol of hope for that long-suffering land so casually given away by Britain to European colonists with a nationalist agenda, in blatant disregard of the rights and interests of its indigenous people. Great powers could do that kind of thing in those days, yet even now they sometimes think they can re-arrange other countries more to their liking. Trans-Jordan (the pre-1949 name for modern Jordan), Aden, Somaliland, Burma, Hong Kong all follow on along this path. Some names we are now unfamiliar with: Perlis, the smallest constituent state of the Federation of Malaysia, lying snugly in its north-west corner, Kalantan likewise lying in the north-eastern part of Malaysia, both abutting Thailand; Penang, an island paradise once delightfully without an airport.

A NOTE ON THE OAK SPECIES REPRESENTING IMPERIAL POSSESSIONS, NEXT TO THE PATH

Q. conferta: otherwise known as the Hungarian oak, a native of south-eastern Europe, introduced to Britain in c.1837.

Q. ilex: the holly oak, a dark tree, always in leaf, is a native of southern Europe, the first specimen introduced to Britain, c.1560, is still alive, in Fulham Palace Gardens. The ubiquity of the holly oak in many great houses is sometimes ascribed to the fact that many English gentlemen toured classical Italy from the sixteenth century onwards, bringing back stone sculptures and furniture, much of which – for want of polystyrene – was packed in local (holly oak) acorns for the journey to Britain. The acorns were thrown out, only to germinate and grow into fully-fledged trees.

Q. lucombeana: the Lucombe oak, is a hybrid between the cork oak (*Q.suber*) and the Turkey oak (*Q. cerris*) produced by a William Lucombe, an Exeter nurseryman in c.1765. It is an unusually vigorous and rapid-growing oak, able to grow seven metres in seven years, hence its commercial attraction as a hardwood timber producer.

Q. macranthera: very large-leafed, is a native of Persia and the Caucasus, introduced in c.1895.

Q. mirbekii: is native to the north African coast and south-western Europe. Introduced to France by the French General Pelissier in c.1845. Pelissier was engaged in the 'pacification' of the Algerian people, a project that left an estimated one million men, women and children dead. As a symbol therefore of what is so often implicit in acquiring an empire, the choice of this species can hardly be faulted. Some of the acorns were subsequently given to Queen Victoria by King Louis Philippe.

Q. palustris: or pin oak, is a native of eastern North America, introduced to Britain in 1800. The leaves often turn deep scarlet in the autumn.

Q. turneri: or Turner's oak, a partial evergreen, is a cross between *Q. ilex* and *Q. robur*, the English or common oak. It was grown in the eighteenth century by Spencer Turner, an Essex nurseryman and remains relatively uncommon.

When you reach the formal avenue lined by young limes (the avenue from Cumberland Lodge) turn left to the Cow Pond.
The Cow Pond was here, albeit in a less geometric shape, when Norden drew his map in 1607, probably originally created to water cattle here. It was probably shaped in about 1700, as part of the landscaping of the lands of the Great (Cumberland) Lodge, perhaps by Sarah Churchill, Duchess of Marlborough, who became Ranger in c.1702 and remained such until 1744, living at the lodge for many years, a home she found 'a thousand times more agreeable than Blenheim'.

As for the Cow Pond, it was very much more formal than it is today, and in the middle years of the eighteenth century a gazebo was designed by Flitcroft, from which to contemplate the pond's murky depths or, more probably, as a quiet spot in which to engage in sweet dalliance. Admire the present one, dated 2015. While surrounded by a young oak plantation, the pond was not hedged in by the impenetrable darkness of rhododendron. They came later, courtesy of George IV. It was he who also planted the rhododendron ride, a rather melancholy route running down the eastern edge of the Great Park from Bishopsgate to the north-east corner of Savill Garden.

Retrace your steps for c.150 metres, until you reach a sandy path leading off to your left. Follow it back to the Savill Visitor's Centre.

The Long Walk and the deer park

WALK 6

Distance 13 or 9km: 3½ or 2½ hours

This walk takes you along the old eastern boundary pale of Windsor Great Park, where it abuts Old Windsor Wood, past Bear's Rails, with an optional stroll up the Long Walk to the gates of the Castle, and back across the foot of Snow Hill.

Start at Bishopsgate.

Bishopsgate Lodge is, as the date over the door indicates, Edwardian. It is a curious, dark building, with heavy bargeboards over the entrance, but not on the other gable ends. One almost suspects this cottage has been constructed out of pirated pieces from elsewhere. Its predecessor, dated c.1830 and designed by Jeffry Wyatville, had stood on the other side of the road.

Enter the park, ignore the riders' gate on your right, but take the next (pedestrian) gate on your right. Turn right again and follow the edge of the riding track. Once you have doubled back towards Bishopsgate, but now inside the deer fence, you will find yourself walking across Cook's Hill and descending a steep slope. You have about 2km alongside the riding track through woodland.

Cook's Hill, which descends to Old Windsor Wood, is marked on John Norden's 1607 map as Combery Hill. Combery may have been a local personality, but it also seems to be the same as the

122 **6** THE LONG WALK AND THE DEER PARK

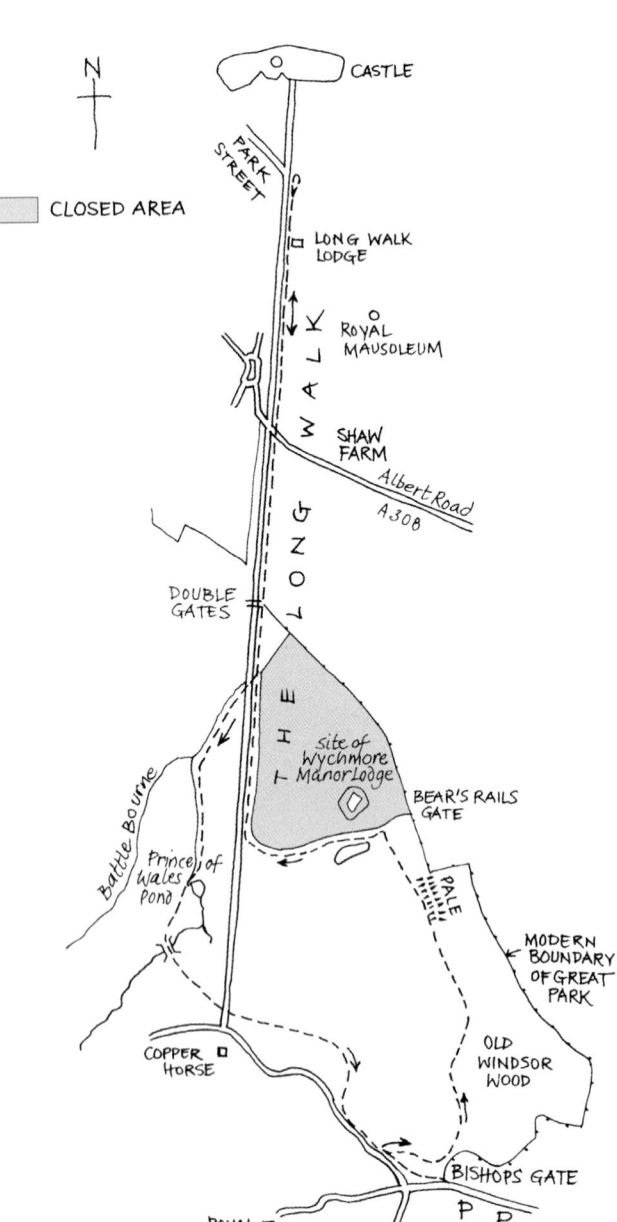

Welsh 'Cymru', for Comber is Old English for Briton. So you may speculate that this was the meaning of the name.

Once the riding track has turned northwards you may notice larch growing on your right, perhaps a mid-twentieth century planting. Larch, one of the few deciduous conifers, became immensely popular for timber yield on large estates, following its introduction from the Alps in the seventeenth century. The Duke of Atholl, for example, planted a mere 14 million over 60 years from 1764.

Behind and indeed after the larch, you are walking through the western margins of Old Windsor Wood, only acquired by the Great Park in the early 1730s. Much of this is ancient woodland and wood pasture, well furnished with veteran trees. Currently the Turkey oak (*Q. cerris*), a fast-growing exotic introduced for its timber yield, is being progressively thinned and the conifers eliminated, to return the area to native woodland. Old Windsor Wood was certainly in existence in 1607 but there is no record of how old it may be. Almost as soon as it was acquired by the Great Park, many trees were felled here for two purposes: to create open rides through the wood, presumably for hunting, and to raise money to fence this new acquisition in. It remained fenced as a separate parcel of land for several decades before being integrated into the park. It was also almost immediately used as a deer park, with 100 red deer released into the wood. This was during a period of over-stocking of the park. In 1735 the Duchess of Marlborough – not known for a placid temper – was complaining 'by His majesty's Directions, a great Quantity of Red Deer are already sent [to the Great Park] and many more are everyday expected.'

By 1800 Nathaniel Kent (see p. 220) had established a wood yard here to produce agricultural and gardening implements for the estate. Furthermore, a brick kiln was established downhill to the east. It was much handier to manufacture bricks on site, for any building work that might be required.

In 1880 the Prince of Wales gifted some wild boar to the park, which were wisely kept in their own enclosure on the slopes of the wood.

The pond you pass down in the gully on your right is modern, a significant aid to the biodiversity of this little frequented part of the park. It has been created where until recently there was a conifer plantation. The area is fenced to protect regeneration of native species from grazing deer.

As the riding track levels out, ignore a track crossing into Old Windsor Wood to the right, and keep walking straight on. This is another area, like Cranbourne, earmarked to be developed as wood pasture. It cries out for similar treatment, too, with the introduction of more longhorn cattle, or some other rare breed which will add delight to the scene, while contributing to the ecology of the area. You may wonder how cattle add value to the landscape. There are two principal ways: they graze more discriminatingly than either deer or sheep, thus allowing certain plant species and particularly seed-heads, to flourish. Furthermore, there will be invertebrates associated specifically with cow dung, thus also increasing biodiversity.

You will pass patches of birch trees. Clearly there has been some tree clearance here, perhaps 40 years ago. Birch always colonises empty ground if the soil is suitably poor, as clearly it is here. Furthermore, the deer must have been denied access to this area at the time that these birches were establishing themselves, otherwise they would have been killed by grazing.

As the tree cover opens out on the right, you may notice (but do not waste time if you do not) about 25m to your right a very low bank, the ancient pale of the Great Park, dividing it from Old Windsor Wood, a small reminder that you are shadowing the perimeter of the medieval deer park. The two estates were united in the later eighteenth century, hence this bank remains distinct, until it runs into the brambles at the back of the housing development that you will see on your right.

On your left is the Boy Scout campsite, first established in 1937.

Continue up the track until you reach the T-junction and pause.
Note two buildings to your right, the first, a pair of semis by Sydney Tatchell (presumably designed at the same time as he was working on the Village (see p. 53) and further to the right the Bear's Rails gate lodge, built in 1866 and almost immediately altered by the architect, Anthony Salvin (for a brief word on him, see p. 94).

Turn left and keep to the track that cleaves to the fencing on the right, pausing when you pass the pond on your left.
This area was once a separate manor, acquired and taken into the Great Park by Edward III in 1359. Bear's Rails is the name in usage probably for the last 500 years, and indicates the kind of creature kept caged here, presumably for the royal amusement. Its previous name, however, was Wychmere, a manor that seems to have run southwards roughly as far as Bishopsgate. The name 'Wychmere' must be Saxon and may well refer to the Hwicce, a major Saxon tribe in the seventh century. 'Mere', indicates a pool here (not necessarily the one on your left, but the name certainly implies there was indeed a pond somewhere around here). Wychmere, or Bear's Rails, has the best surviving moat in the Great Park, but is sadly inaccessible. It lies on your right, 100m across the open field, in a grove of trees. (For more about moats of this period, see p. 22.) Edward seems to have refurbished

the manor house as a second hunting lodge, but it did not last for long, being demolished some time before 1400.

If you have not already seen deer during this walk you are almost bound to do so soon, and you may wish to read the section on deer parks (pp.192-197). Deer hunting took place over some of this terrain. George III continued the tradition of stag hunting, but apparently not frequently. Prince Albert also took the Royal Buckhounds out hunting in the Great Park. The deer were always an enticement to theft. In 1841 a long suspected poacher, Joseph Atkins, also known as Lovely Joe, was caught red-handed very close to Bear's Rails. As *The Times* reported from the first hearing, at about 1.30am in the morning of 1 August, a team of keepers

> 'heard the report of a gun about 300 yards from where they were standing. After waiting quietly behind trees for nearly half an hour, they saw the prisoner [Atkins] descend from the wall into the park, by means of a short ladder… It was from the top of this wall the deer was shot. The fellow, in attempting to carry off the deer, several times tried to get it upon his shoulders, but failed, from the state of drunkenness he was in, falling each time with the deer in his arms… The prisoner, who said nothing in his defence, was fully committed… to take his trial for the capital offence of killing and slaying a deer within enclosed grounds… at the next assizes for the county of Berks.'

If you wish to know whether he swung for his crime, was transported for life or was given a more lenient punishment, you will have to check the Berkshire assize records. So, if you intend to break the law, be warned: inebriation is best avoided.

During the Second World War the deer herd was largely dispersed, principally in order to maximise agriculture. In 1950 it was announced that all remaining deer in the Great Park would also be disposed of. It was only with the return of much farmland to parkland in 1979, that the Great Park was restocked with deer from Balmoral.

Continue walking with the fencing close by on your right. When you reach the Long Walk, turn right and read as you go. After 500m, watch out for a line of oaks coming in from the left, and the tops of brick culverts, marking the course of the Battle Bourne. If you do not wish to walk the length of the Long Walk, turn to ⊃ on p.136.

Charles II only embarked upon the Long Walk in 1680, a full decade after he had repossessed the Great Park from those who took parcels of it during the Commonwealth. A royal warrant was issued,

> 'by reason that the King is disposed to have an avenue 240 feet broad made in direct line between our Castle of Windsor and our Great Park there.'

He therefore authorised his officers to approach those tenants whose land was in the way and to make them an offer they could not, or dare not, refuse. Yet there are limits to force majeure even for a King. Charles felt unable to oust one or two tenants, most notably his very own mistress, Nell Gwynn and her children, who lived at Burford House close to the southern perimeter of the Castle. There was therefore a dogleg of open lawn for the final 350m or so, up to the south-east corner of the Castle. By 1683 virtually all the necessary land acquisitions for the rest of the Walk were completed, and the planting of the whole avenue with a double row of English elms, 1,652 trees no less, was completed by the time of his death in February 1685. Where the Long Walk crossed the Battle Bourne, a brick culvert was built to ensure that the avenue was uninterrupted.

The Long Walk was inspired by the work of Le Nôtre at

Versailles. Le Nôtre set the standard to which every garden-minded European monarch tried to aspire. Without a carriageway until the early eighteenth century it was intended essentially as a vista and as a route for mounted, not wheeled, traffic. A gravelled road was laid to accommodate Queen Anne, whose fondness for the chase was compromised by the chronic rheumatism to which she had fallen victim even before she ascended the throne at the age of 37. Riding on horseback had long become impossible and she hunted in her chaise. As with her eponymous Ride, Queen Anne was able to drive to the scenes of hunting, normally beyond the Great Park in Cranbourne or Windsor Forest further south.

It was not until the early nineteenth century that the Long Walk was completed all the way up to the Castle. It was George IV who was the driving force behind the aesthetic completion of this great avenue, along with the Copper Horse (p.108).

By the 1840s the original trees were some 160 years old, and some were replaced. Following a major review of the whole avenue in the late 1850s, a programme of replanting was commenced in 1879. Elms were retained at the north end, where they would enjoy the soil, which is loam on chalk, while the southern part of the avenue was replanted with oak trees, which would do better than elm because the soil here turns to gravel on clay. The oak saplings were grown close by, from indigenous stock, but needed twenty years' successful growth before being ready for replanting on the Long Walk itself.

With a serious outbreak of elm disease, it was decided in 1943 to fell all the trees including the few original elms. The avenue was replanted with London planes for the outer row, and horse chestnuts for the inner row, in the words of the then Royal Librarian, 'so that in 30 years' time one or other can be eliminated and the more successful variety left. It is a correct decision,

Felling the elms of the Long Walk in 1943, the whole job done by hand, with a two-man crosscut saw.

lament it as we may.' During thinning in the 1970s both species were retained but now nature may have intervened to make the decision for us. The non-native horse chestnut is currently under stress from three sources. Summer droughts, perhaps the pattern of the future, have reduced the strength and health of trees. Bleeding canker, with the visible symptom of black gummy liquid which oozes through the bark, can kill a tree, by destroying the *phloem* of the inner bark, which takes the starch down to the root system. It has been spreading northwards in the past five years, perhaps a symptom of climate change but it is an ill still poorly understood. Finally the horse chestnut leaf miner moth attacks the leaf. The moth has virtually no predators, so it thrives and multiplies. The moth lays its eggs on the leaf and when the eggs hatch, the larvae 'mine' into the leaf, making their home between the upper and lower skins of the leaf. The chrysalis over-winters within fallen foliage. When the moth hatches in April it swarms the tree trunk before laying eggs on the tops of leaves, and the cycle thus continues. It is not clear yet whether these three assaults on horse chestnut health will prove generally fatal.

Proceed to the Double Gates.

You will immediately be wondering why 'double'? The term refers to the fact that there were once two sets of gates on this edge of the Great Park, one to the north of the other. A public road ran in between the two sets of gates, from Clewer Green in the west to Englefield Green, east of the Great Park.

As you proceed northwards, out of the Great Park, look out for the hawthorn hedge on either side of the Long Walk.

Because there were deer and other livestock roaming around, a bank was raised on either side of the original Long Walk, on which two rows of quicksett, or hawthorn as we now call it, were grown. Hawthorn – meaning in Saxon, 'hedge' or 'enclosure' thorn – was the longstanding favourite for hedging. Wholly manmade hedges are almost invariably dominated by hawthorn, but it is the older hedgerows, sometimes lines of surviving trees from felled woodland, or ones between fields that grew by neglect, which contain a much greater variety of species. Here you find a hawthorn hedge lining the avenue, growing at exactly the same width, 240 feet, as the original double hedge that ran the length of the Long Walk in Charles II's time.

To your left, across the fields, you will see a large brick complex. This is Queen's Gate, built in 1952, the clock tower in 1960, to accommodate staff of the Crown Estate.

Cross the Albert Road.

The old Windsor-Datchet road had run across from Park Street under the walls of the Castle and across what is now Home Park, thus separating Frogmore, then in the hands of a commoner, from the Castle and adjacent grounds. With its acquisition of Frogmore the royal family was anxious to remove this public road, and by act of Parliament it was re-routed here in 1851, and named Albert Road. The diversion also involved removing the old bridge across the Thames to Datchet and throwing a new one across further downstream.

On your right stands Shaw Farm, now also part of the Crown Estate. Prince Albert took over the farm and completely revamped it as a 'Model Farm' with state of the art buildings. These were demolished in the late 1970s, to be replaced with buildings better suited to late twentieth century farming methods. The farm remains home to the Queen's pedigree Ayrshire herd.

Just before you pass Long Walk Gate look out for a plaque against the railings on your right.

This plaque need not detain you unless you are interested either in aviation or philately. Shaw Farm meadow, beyond the railings, is the site of the landing of the first aerial postal flight in September 1911, commemorating the coronation of George V. The pilot was Gustav Hamel, one of those magnificent men, and he had only been flying for six months. He had learnt to fly at Louis Blériot's school of aviation at Pau, at the foot of the Pyrenees, taking his very first flight in March that year. So he was hardly a veteran when he made the 21-mile flight from Hendon to Windsor in barely ten minutes. If you possess one of the commemorative postcards he carried on that flight, you probably keep it in the bank safe. They are rarities of philately. As for Hamel, he disappeared during a flight over the English Channel in May 1914. Foul play – German machinations – was suspected, and after war broke out, because his father was a distinguished German physician, there were silly rumours that Hamel had

6 THE LONG WALK AND THE DEER PARK

flown to Germany to lead bombing raids on England. There can be little doubt of the prosaic truth that he had simply crashed into the sea and drowned.

Look out also for Long Walk Gate Lodge, on your right.
This plain but elegant lodge was built in 1854 for the gate keeper of a new access road laid in 1851 to the south end of the Home Park, on the Castle's eastern flank, and the north end of Frogmore. Enjoy the lion heads on the soffit boards.

Approach the Castle.
There is a real irony in the need for modern defences to an ancient castle. Those who built the early defences of the castle would have loved the retractable vehicle traps set behind the gate, one can almost hear their gasp of admiration for such a cunning and elegant device. What you now see of the castle is almost entirely the work of Jeffry Wyatville for George IV (see p.112). William the Conqueror first chose the site as part of a ring of defences around the approaches to London. These castles, now virtually all either ruined or disappeared, were at Berkamsted, Hertford, Ongar, Rayleigh, Rochester, Tonbridge, Reigate

THE LONG WALK AND THE DEER PARK 6 133

The south front of Windsor Castle, Elias Ashmole, The Antiquities of Berkshire, *1719.*

and Guildford. Initially they were all, including the fortress at Windsor, wooden palisades. Windsor, commenced c.1070, was incontestably the most important of these, partly because the site, on a chalk outcrop, was so superb but more importantly because it overlooked the Thames, easily the principal highway for the movement of goods and people in southern England. The fortress was composed of a fortified mound or motte, now the site of the Round Tower, and a lower and upper bailey, two open areas surrounded by palisades. Henry II rebuilt in stone in around 1170. He used chalk as convenient infill, but the exterior was built in extremely durable heath, or sarsen, stone, excavated on Bagshot Heath (for more on this stone see p. 87).

Turn back down the Long Walk.

Look out on your left for glimpses of the green copper roof of the Royal Mausoleum in Frogmore. Albert was only four days dead in December 1861 when a mausoleum in Frogmore was decided upon. The architect was Albert Humbert, who had come to royal notice because he was commissioned to rebuild the chancel of the church on the Isle of Wight, which the Royal Family attended while at Osborne. Humbert had already designed one mausoleum at Frogmore, for the Queen's mother the Duchess of Kent. On that occasion it was inspired by Hawksmoor's great mausoleum at Castle Howard. But the Royal Mausoleum is considered his masterpiece, a central dome on a Latin cross plan with a Romanesque exterior. It was not finished until 1871, when at last Albert came to his resting place. Humbert went on to Sandringham, which Edward Prince of Wales had acquired in 1862, and rebuilt it. If you have not already done so, look out for the infrequent occasions on which the Royal Mausoleum is open to the public. The tomb inside is the work of Carlo Giovanni Marochetti, a Sardinian by origin. You will have seen his work before, for he it was who wrought the statue of Richard I outside the Palace of Westminster.

Retrace your steps through the Double Gates.
On your right lies the Review Ground, during Queen Victoria's reign the scene of many military reviews. Martial gatherings in the Great Park have a long pedigree, dating back to the Middle Ages (see p. 193). This land had previously been known as Fussey Meadow, perhaps a corruption of 'furzey' meadow, a landscape dominated by furze or gorse. In 1844, Czar Nicholas I of Russia reviewed troops here. In 1855 it was the turn of the Empress Eugénie while her husband, the Emperor Napoleon III, rode 'a very fiery beautiful chestnut called Philips', on which he charged alongside the cavalry. How like the knightly gatherings of Edwards I and III. Sure enough, the following day Victoria invested Napoleon as Knight of the Garter, the very order inaugurated by King Edward at Windsor in 1348. In truth, Victoria had been swept away by the charm of this tubby and visually unprepossessing man.

In 1873 Queen Victoria held a review in honour of Nasr ad-

Dragoons gallop past their sovereign.

Din Shah of Persia. Nasr ad-Din was one of the more capable of the late Qajar shahs. Nevertheless he reigned over an empire weakened by the centrifugal effect of recalcitrant and often rebellious tribal confederations. Indeed, his small standing army was dependent on supplementation by unreliable tribal irregulars. His empire was under relentless pressure on his northern frontiers. Russia had progressively seized the cities of the central Asian khanates to the north: Tashkent in 1866, Samarqand in 1868 and Khiva in 1873. Nasr al-Din Shah badly needed British support, but he also feared it. Britain had its own appetite for strategic bases. It must therefore have been with mixed feelings of envy, fear and possibly even hope, that he watched 8,000 disciplined troops strut their stuff on the Review Ground. As Victoria noted, he was particularly impressed by the batteries of light artillery, the Highlanders and skirmishing riflemen. However, as an act of diplomacy, the review came to nothing. The Persians soon discovered how indifferent the British could be to

6 THE LONG WALK AND THE DEER PARK

George V and Lord Baden-Powell review the Boy Scouts, Coronation celebration, 1911

their problems. As the Persian envoy stated the following year: 'Where they [the Persians] looked for sympathy they had only met with coldness & indifference.'

⬤ About 350m after the Double Gates, watch out for the course of the Battle Bourne, running off to your right (or on your left after about 750m if you have decided to skip the Long Walk up to the Castle), marked by the tops of a series of low brick culverts and the line of oak trees. Turn off the Long Walk to follow the Battle Bourne westwards, keeping to the left side of the stream, which is now completely channelled in a brick culvert.

The Battle Bourne, clearly marked on Norden's map, rises on the high ground on the west side of the park, from Cranbourne to Sandpit Gate. (For the name origin, see p. 46.)

After 250m the Battle Bourne divides. Take the left fork, but follow the path on the right of the stream which leads you up to Prince of Wales Pond. Turn right when you reach the pond, but

just before the track begins to peter out, veer off slightly left of the track, and make for what looks like fencing in the line of trees. When you reach the Battle Bourne again, avoid the horse jumps and cross it either by the small bridge or by scrambling down across the gully.

You may wonder where you are being taken. In fact this part of the walk is intended to take you in a wide arc away from the hard grind of walking straight down the Long Walk, of which you have probably done enough, and to take you through a more interesting landscape, one that generates a sense of well being.

Once across the stream veer diagonally left and keep close to the rising ground on your right but do not climb it. Cross the Long Walk below the Copper Horse and the tarmac carriageway beneath it. Make your way through this wonderful landscape, slowly edging up the rising ground to your right.

Here at last, you are in the English Elysium itself, England's pleasant pastures green, adorned with those priceless treasure houses, the veteran oaks. The treasure, of course, is the extraordinary range of wildlife hosted by a veteran oak. On your left you may notice a line of mature oaks, marking a track that existed here in the mid-nineteenth century. As they age, these trees will host an increasing range of diverse life.

Watch out for a gap in the trees on the hillside on your right, for at some point you must climb the hill to join the less interesting route of the tarmac carriageway that takes you back to the deer fence gate by the Royal Lodge, and thus out to Bishopsgate.

The gardens of Windsor Great Park

There is a map on page 150 for the Valley Gardens, and a list of what to look out for each month on p.152. It is planned to have more information on the Valley Gardens available at the Visitors' Centre in future. In the case of the Savill Garden, a monthly map comes with your ticket, indicating the principal plants of interest that month.

Unlike the rest of the Great Park, there is no prescribed route for a walk. Go and look at what appeals to you. At the end of the section there are short background pieces written about some of the more prominent exotic flora that one can enjoy in the gardens, principally concerning the history of their introduction to Britain:

(a) azaleas (p.167);
(b) camellias (p.170);
(c) conifers (p.172),
(d) hydrangeas in Walk No. 3 (p.177)
(e) magnolias (p.178);
(f) rhododendrons (p.178).

I hope that these will whet your appetite to look again at plants which you may in the past have taken for granted, and also to hold in some respect those who risked their lives to find them.

INTRODUCTION

These publicly accessible gardens, the Savill and Valley Gardens, are the most significant examples in Britain of mid-twentieth century gardening on the grand scale. They are located in the south-eastern part of the park, almost exclusively in that part falling within the county of Surrey.

The reason for this location lies in the geology of the landscape. For while the northern and western parts of the park are largely chalk, clay and loam, this area is covered with sand, known as Bagshot Sand, with a few patches of clay. This sand is nutrient-poor acid soil, virtually lime free. Among the plants that can be grown in such poor soil are rhododendrons, camellias, heathers and conifers.

Well-drained sandy soil, of course, is also perfect for rabbit warrens. The earliest map we have of Windsor Great Park, made by John Norden in 1607, marks the high ground at the top of the Valley Gardens as 'White Cony borrowe hill', and half a century later another map labels it 'Conny Warren'. (The word 'coney' began to fall into disuse about 200 years ago, in favour of 'rabbit', previously used only of the young.)

ERIC SAVILL

For the creation of these gardens, we are indebted to a passionate gardener, Eric Savill (1895-1980). Savill learnt horticulture at his mother's knee, for when she was not busy campaigning for women's rights, she was a keen and skilful landscape gardener. He was set to join the family firm of estate surveyors and agents (today one of the most prominent in the land). At Cambridge he shared lodgings with Owen Morshead, who later became Librarian of Windsor Castle. On the outbreak of war, Savill abandoned his degree course and joined up. In 1916 he was wounded on the Somme and would have died except for the exceptional and sustained valour of one of his men who made five attempts to retrieve him under fire. (We all owe Private Theodore Veale vc a debt of gratitude and it is nice to know that he himself died at the ripe old age of 89.) After the war Savill returned to Cambridge and then joined the family firm where he became

Sir Eric Savill (right) in attendance as the Queen plants a tree.

experienced in estate management. In the meantime he was a frequent weekend visitor to his friend Morshead, now at Windsor, and got to know the landscape well. So it may not have been wholly out of the blue – though it seemed so at the time – that in 1931 he was offered the post of deputy surveyor at Windsor. This involved management of 15,000 acres of farmland, woodland and parkland stretching from Windsor to Bagshot.

The story and description of each garden is set out below. Their creation required determination, flair, an understanding of plants and a highly skilled use of the landscape. Furthermore, they required the ability to scrounge and cajole when funding was unavailable. There is something very engaging about this man of unassailable probity cadging plants for free wherever possible. Here was someone with a mission and nothing would stand in his way. Knighted in 1955, he died in 1980.

Savill's gardens are quintessentially twentieth century, with their most defining quality being the absence of straight lines. Think in your mind's eye of the royal gardens at Hampton Court, laid out in the 1690s, and then of the Valley Gardens, laid out in the 1940s. They are so profoundly different they hardly bear comparison. The former bears a powerful message of Man in dominion over nature, turning nature's 'chaos' into controlled order, its patterns resembling a carpet or tapestry. It was a platform on which Man could strut his stuff. In contrast, Savill's approach is a natural development from the English landscaped garden. This had been based upon vistas that led the eye to admire the shapes and perspectives of nature, in shades of green. Savill used the exotic discoveries of the late eighteenth and nineteenth centuries, particularly those from Asia, to replace green with riotous colour. Planting with colour demanded fresh skills to ensure a harmonious rather than cacophonous outcome.

You may be interested in some of Savill's ploys to achieve the right effect. His paths and vistas responded to the contours of the landscape. He never planted in even numbers lest the plants looked regimented, but always clusters of three, five, seven and so forth. Nor would he ever ring the base of a tree with planting. He might plant a drift up to a tree, or away from it, but he almost always ensured the base of the tree was partially visible. Nor would he over-plant the front of a bed, but always carry the eye back by taking the planting among background trees. Finally, he ensured there were bold verticals, provided by mature trees. Sadly, most of us do not possess rolling acres behind our semi-detached home to make use of such cunning tips.

THE SAVILL BUILDING, THE VISITORS' CENTRE

Opened in the summer of 2006 this building is, in the words of its architect, Glenn Howells, 'almost a piece of garden furniture'. The wood for the roof and floors almost all comes from the Windsor Estate's woodland, much of it developed by Eric Savill himself seventy years ago. The roof is a 'gridshell', composed of two layers of interlocking larch laths, supported by its own double curvature. The underside of the roof contains 400 larch trees from the estate, topped by 30cm of insulation and weatherproofing and oak from the sustainable woodlands of Cranbourne in the Great Park, on the exterior. The roof is over 90m in length and up to 25m wide. Over 400 larch trees from the Crown Estate were used.

THE SAVILL GARDEN

Within a year of his appointment, Savill had proposed laying out a woodland garden that would be accessible to the general public and, with the assent of the Royal Family, was able to proceed. The area he chose was overgrown with *Rhododendron ponticum*, laurel, elder and bracken, all of them difficult to eradicate. But it still boasted fine oaks and beeches planted by the Duke of Cumberland as a boundary belt, c.1750. It took a skilled eye to decide which trees merited preservation as features within the future garden. A ditch was dug to drain the area and to form a stream and a pond (the Upper Pond), which was created along its flow. What the pond needed, of course, was marsh marigolds and flag iris. Savill mentioned this lack to the park foreman, who promptly went off on his bicycle, with a basket of rabbits on his handlebars. As Savill anticipated, the foreman returned some hours later with a basketful of marsh marigolds, still dripping from their recent home, a triumph of the barter economy. The marsh marigold, or king-cup, should be cherished. It is one of our most ancient native species, probably predating the Great Ice Age. It used to be common on agricultural land, but is increasingly a garden plant because of relentless drainage of the countryside.

Another early feature of the Savill Gardens was the mauve and purple primula, *Primula denticulata*. We owe this Himalayan

Clearing the ground for the Savill Garden.

plant to a physician of the East India Company, John Royle, who introduced it to Britain in 1837. The ones here, or rather their forebears, were not even bartered for. They were skilfully cadged. One day, Savill found himself in St James' Park, chatting with the Superintendent there. 'Mr Hay,' Savill enquired, 'what becomes of the primulas when they are lifted from the park to make way for summer bedding?' A fortnight later a lorry-load of unwanted primulas arrived at Savill's woodland garden. The garden also began to acquire camellias and woodland lilies, initially mostly donated.

And so the garden grew until it reached its present extent of 35 acres, with many gifts from Savill's gardening friends and acquaintances, the boundaries of the garden enlarged and the Lower Pond, which already existed, excavated and dredged of the silt of many years. One of the more notable donors was Lionel de Rothschild, who grew rhododendrons in his gardens at Exbury, on the Beaulieu estuary. De Rothschild loved to share his delight in the species. After lunch his guests would find themselves handed a sable-haired brush, paper-bags, labels on which to put their name and then invited to cross-pollinate any rhododendron of their choice, covering the pollinated flowers with a bag bearing their name. Some months later such guests would receive a pan of seedlings, de Rothschild's gardeners having collected, sown and pricked out the results of cross-pollination.

At the upper end of the garden lie the herbaceous borders and rose beds. A specimen of the Willow Podocarp (*Podocarpus salignus*) with its multiple trunks grows in the middle of the lawn, the happy consequence of an abandoned box of seedlings which took root before the garden here was established. Among conifers, the *Podocarpus* genus contains the second largest number of species. This species was introduced from the Chilean Andes in 1853. Most podocarp species grow in the southern hemisphere.

One of the intriguing features of early plants is their disposition around the globe. The Podocarpus genus is very largely confined to the southern hemisphere while the whole Araucariaceae family (which includes the monkey puzzle tree) is exclusively southern hemisphere. As a result such old tree forms hint at the earliest movement of land masses in the early history of the earth, long before dinosaurs, when the earth's lands were clustered around the south pole and Laurasia broke away to form the land masses of the northern hemisphere, and Gondwanaland formed Africa and most of the southern hemisphere.

Beyond the lawn, look out for the arc of five magnificent Monterey pines (*P. radiata*), one of many true pines introduced by the collector David Douglas (see p.176) in 1833, the result of his explorations in California. This tree's only natural location is around Monterey, to which it was probably driven by the Ice Age. When the climate grew warmer, however, it failed to spread beyond Monterey. It is therefore all the more remarkable that, as a result of human propagation, it is set to become a major timber tree of the international market during this century, probably displacing the Douglas fir.

A number of witch hazels (*Hamamelis*) have been planted in the garden. Most of these are from the Far East, but the earliest known species to Europeans, *H. virginiana*, had been found in the late seventeenth century by John Banister (see p.167). It was already well known to Native Americans as a panacea for bruising and for sore or damaged eyes, and we still rely on what they knew then. For a few years during the mid-twentieth century, Optrex established 14 hectares of witch hazel near Basingstoke, of which 2.5 ha were coppiced annually, yielding 133,000 litres distilled liniment. The Basingstoke coppice may have gone but the recipe is still very much in use.

The Wall was erected at the northern end of the garden in 1951, made from bricks recovered from London bombed sites. These too were cadged and the wall itself constructed using estate labour. The wall with its buttresses gives shelter and warmth to exotics that need plenty of sun and also shelter from cold winds. In the same year the woodland garden acquired its present name, a tribute by George VI to the man who had created it.

The Queen Elizabeth Temperate House, opened in 1995, hosts a small collection of tree ferns. If you are remotely interested in the early history of plants and trees, these should command your attention and your respect.

Here is a brief chronology to put tree ferns into context:
3.5bn years ago   first living organisms on Earth: single cell algae, the kind that still makes your pond turn green.

500m years ago   single cell algae have developed into multi-cellular organisms, with potential for cell specialisation.

450m years ago   first evidence of multi-cell algae adapting to life on the land rather than in water: mosses and liverworts, still doing well, the former constantly threatening your lawn.

420m years ago   other plant forms develop columns of cells that can pump nutrients and also the lignin that gives cells the rigidity to acquire height and survive dryness. The earliest tree forms were giant club mosses, which could grow to 40 metres, but they are now extinct. Their fossilised remains turned into coal.

400m years ago   emergence of ferns and tree ferns, our oldest surviving tree form.

Ferns reproduce through spores, released from spore cases. These spores send out a small shoot that grows into a rudimentary plant. This organism contains male and female cells, which fuse to form an embryo fern. But this can only happen in highly propitious damp circumstances. It was another 40 million years before the appearance of plants that reproduced not by spores but by seeds. In the words of the botanist Colin Tudge, 'Spores are like children setting out on a wild adventure with nothing but high spirits and a bag of toffees.' Unlike spores, seeds go forth equipped with carbohydrates, protein and fat for an arduous adventure. Seed plants first appeared about 360 million years ago, 150 million years before the first dinosaurs. Among these, conifers (see p.172) appeared about 300 million years ago. So stand in awe of these tree ferns, the true Ancients of the Earth. Against all the odds, their bags of toffees and their high spirits got them through.

THE VALLEY GARDENS

A BRIEF HISTORY

Eric Savill had wanted to increase the amount of publicly accessible garden but he now had to wait until the end of the war. He thus had plenty of time to select a suitable site and he chose the numerous sandy gullies descending from Smith's Lawn down to Virginia Water, with the right acid soil, plenty of sunshine and plenty of shelter from cold winds. The site, of course, was overgrown with natural vegetation: birch, which is always quick to colonise open patches of acidic soil, as well as bracken. In addition there had been introductions of beech, oak and sweet chestnut by the Duke of Cumberland, and also ponticum rhododendrons planted a little later as game coverts.

The first garden was created in the Main Valley. The terrain was such a jungle that the first workers, recently demobbed from service against the Japanese, called it 'Upper Burma'. By 1947 the site had been cleared, except for certain trees, oaks, beeches, sweet chestnuts and conifers, which were judiciously saved to provide partial shade and height for the rhododendron and azalea shrubberies. Rhododendrons may be quite the most attention-seeking plants here, yet it would be wrong to think of these gardens as devoted solely to rhododendron species. Within the framework of pre-existing mature trees, Savill selected a wide variety of other genera, most notably *Prunus*, *Sorbus*, *Acer*

Clearing 'Upper Burma' in the Valley Gardens.

and *Quercus* and a variety of conifers. The sides of the valley at the lower end near Virginia Water are pure sand with a tendency to be hot and dry. These therefore were planted with cistuses, hypericums, brooms, heaths, potentillas and yuccas.

Savill was operating in a cash-strapped environment of post-war austerity. In the spring of 1949 quite by chance he visited an estate recently belonging to a now deceased specialist in azaleas and rhododendrons. The estate had been bought by an industrial firm. As Savill himself recalled,

> 'an enquiry was made as to whether this firm would care to consider the sale of certain selected plants for transference to Windsor Great Park, a short note of our ambitions being included with the enquiry. It was indeed a surprise when the answer came back that the firm would not consider selling any plants, but that they would be delighted to give all that were of interest to our project.'

(continues on page 154)

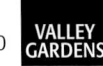

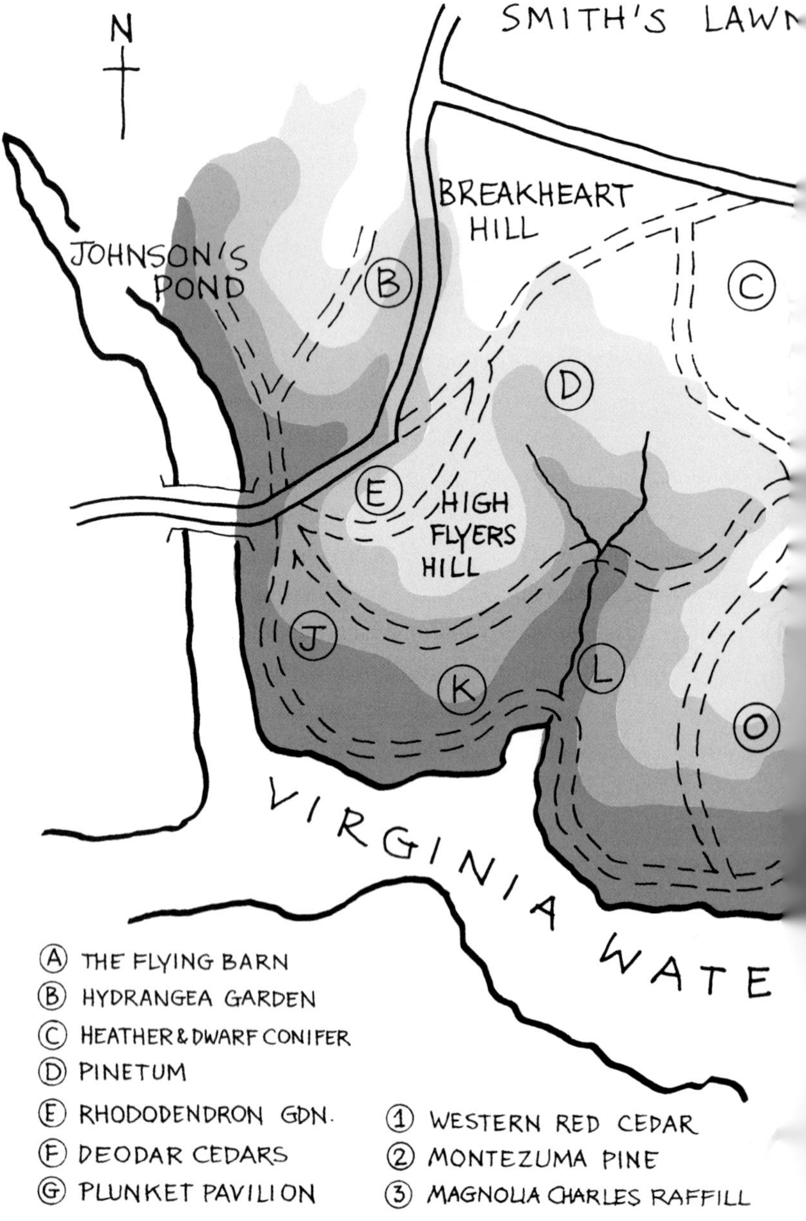
N
SMITH'S LAWN
BREAKHEART HILL
JOHNSON'S POND
HIGH FLYERS HILL
VIRGINIA WATE
B
C
D
E
J
K
L
O
Ⓐ THE FLYING BARN
Ⓑ HYDRANGEA GARDEN
Ⓒ HEATHER & DWARF CONIFER
Ⓓ PINETUM
Ⓔ RHODODENDRON GDN.
Ⓕ DEODAR CEDARS
Ⓖ PLUNKET PAVILION
① WESTERN RED CEDAR
② MONTEZUMA PINE
③ MAGNOLIA CHARLES RAFFILL

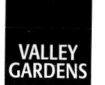

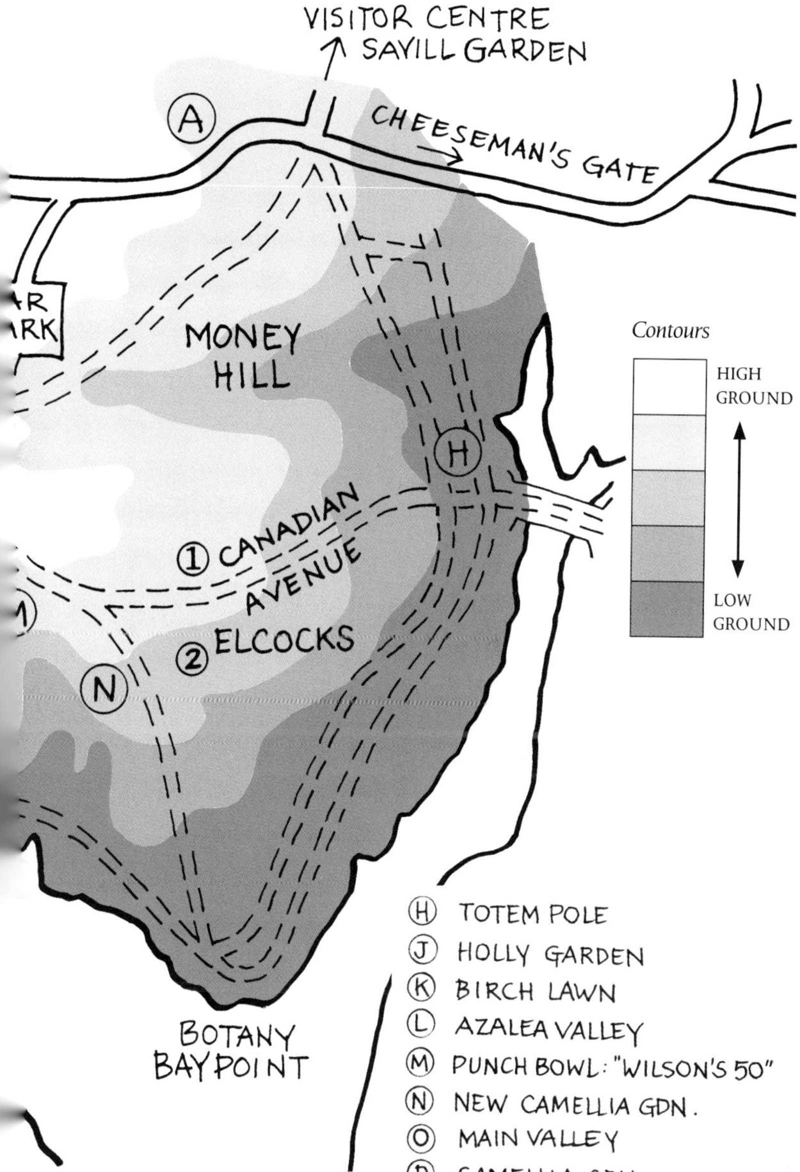
VISITOR CENTRE
SAVILL GARDEN
A
CHEESEMAN'S GATE
MONEY HILL
H
1 CANADIAN AVENUE
2 ELCOCKS
N
BOTANY BAY POINT
Contours
HIGH GROUND
LOW GROUND
H TOTEM POLE
J HOLLY GARDEN
K BIRCH LAWN
L AZALEA VALLEY
M PUNCH BOWL: "WILSON'S 50"
N NEW CAMELLIA GDN.
O MAIN VALLEY
P CAMELLIA GDN.

NOTE OF TREES AND SHRUBS TO LOOK OUT FOR, BY SEASON.

Some species here have their own commentary, as indicated.

January & February
Hamamelis Six species, all have long yellow petals, on *H. virginiata*, see p.164.

Mahonias Seventy species, all with yellow flowers followed by blue-black berries, named after an American horticulturist, Bernard M'Mahon (d.1816).

Parrotia persica Deciduous, it can grow up to 12 m high, flowers have conspicuous red stamens Native of Caucasus, introduced c.1841.

March *Camellias* See p.170. Many varieties.

April *Magnolias* See p.178. Many varieties located in the Main Valley, e.g. *M.dawsonia* up to 12 m. high, petals white streaked, tinged rosy purple, discovered W. Sichuan, 1908 and introduced by Ernest Wilson, 1919. On High Flyers Hill *M. denudata* ('Yulan') up to 9 m high, pure white flowers, introduced 1789, cultivated by the Chinese for at least 1,300 years. Many other varieties here also. One of the most notable is 'Charles Raffill', this is a cross dated 1946, one of the originals to be found on the spur overlooking the west side of the Punch Bowl.

May	Rhododendrons & azaleas See pp.167, 178.
	Davidia involucrata Also known as 'handkerchief tree', 12-20 m high, it is native to W.China. It has strong scented flowers, with large creamy bracts hooded over flower. Named after Abbé David in 1869, but only introduced in 1901 by Ernest Wilson (see p.169). It can be found at the top of the Main Valley, on the east side.
	Enkianthus Ten species, with white or creamy flowers, native to North East Asia.
	Japanese cherries The best known, 'Kanzan' is very common, but here you can find many hybrids.
June	Rhododendrons See p.178.
July	Hydrangeas See p.177.
August & September	Rowans in the Heather and Dwarf Conifer Garden.
October	Acers Or maple, among which are the Norwegian (*A. Platanoides*) and N. American red (*A. rubrum*), silver (*A. saccarhinum*) and sugar maples (*A. saccharum*) as well as Asian varieties, including snake-barked maples.
November	*Parrotia persica* Beautiful tints of gold and crimson foliage.
December	as for January.

By 1951 the main valley, the original core of the gardens, extending over 25 acres was complete. Little by little the garden spread westwards to what became the **Azalea Valley**. These azaleas grow beneath an array of magnolias, flowering cherries, and crab apples.

Since then the gardens have continued to expand into each fresh gully to both west and east. Today the gardens extend over approximately 200 acres, eight times the size of the original concept.

On the north slope of Breakheart Hill, to the west of the road leading to Blacknest Gate and opposite the beginning of the Species Collection of Rhododendrons is a broad planting of matsumu hybrids, progressively displacing Sargeant's Cherry (*Prunus sargentii*), a Japanese species introduced in 1890.

A Kanzan cherry plantation, east of the Valley Gardens, lies on the hillside near the head of a ride flanked by copper beeches and snowy medlars, an approach for those visiting the Valley Gardens from the Obelisk/Savill Gardens car park. Japanese cherry trees were introduced as early as 1822, but the 'Kanzan' cultivar arrived almost a century later, in c.1913, dismissed sniffily by one expert as 'a poorly shaped dull plant all summer'. So either catch it in bud (April) or in flower (May), or wait till the autumn when the trees are luminous gold and pink. As for the copper beeches, the same expert writes:

'…. they flush brownish-pink but soon assume the heavy, dark, blackish purple colour which disfigures so much of our landscape. Grossly overplanted in villages, rectory gardens, churchyards, parks and all commemorative plantings. Only 'River's Purple' a superior dark red form can, occasionally be excused.'

So do not for a moment think of flora as uncontroversial. Just as some kindle love, others raise the bile.

WHERE TO WALK?

You must decide for yourself where you wish to go. Brief notes follow on some of the locations, followed by notes on plant genera and species that are important in these gardens.

Locations	Main Valley	p.148
	Azalea Valley	p.154
	The Punch Bowl	p.155
	The Rhododendron Garden	p.156
	The Hydrangea Garden	p.70
	The Heather and dwarf conifer garden	p.157
	The Pinetum	p.159
	The Totem Pole	p.162
Plant genera and species	Azaleas	p.167
	Camellias	p.170
	Conifers	p.172
	Hydrangeas	p.177
	Magnolias	p.178
	Rhododendrons	p.178

THE PUNCH BOWL

The Azalea Punch Bowl is the most spectacular part of the Valley Gardens when in bloom. If you enjoy azaleas, it is worth walking around the paths, not merely looking either from below or above. It is here that most of the 'Wilson Fifty' Kurume azaleas are on display (on azaleas and Ernest Wilson, see p.169). It was Jack Stevenson (see below) in 1946 who first exclaimed, 'What a wonderful site in which to grow Kurume azaleas.' He also promised to provide the 'Wilson Fifty', or rather all except those insufficiently hardy. Cuttings were taken and by 1950 over 50,000 specimens were actually planted. Great skill has been used to ensure that the wide range of colours does not actually clash. Furthermore some shade and height was achieved by punctuating the array of azaleas with maples, snowbell trees (*Styrax japonica*) and enkianthus shrubs, all from Japan, within an existing framework of larch and noble firs (*Abies procera*).

THE RHODODENDRON GARDEN

The genesis of this garden was the death of one of the most renowned British rhododendron experts, Jack Barr Stevenson, in 1950. Stevenson had been a highly successful business magnate. He and his wife had purchased Tower Court, a house in extensive grounds on a woody ridge between Ascot and Bagshot in 1918, and started to transform the lawns into a dedicated collection of rhododendron species. It was intended to provide a systematic inventory of species. By the time of Stevenson's death in 1950, Tower Court boasted the most complete collection in the world. Stevenson himself had edited *The Species of Rhododendron* (1930), the species bible of its time. Stevenson's collection included plants raised from seed sent back to Britain by the great rhododendron hunters of their day: Wilson (p.169), Farrer, Forrest (p.179) and Kingdon-Ward (p.184). His widow decided to sell the collection as a whole. When word reached George VI, he immediately resolved on the acquisition of the collection, for rhododendrons were his favourite plant. But it was a time of post-war austerity and the Treasury initially objected to the sum Mrs Stevenson, herself almost broke, required. We do not know quite what George VI said to Hugh Gaitskell, Chancellor of the Exchequer, but whatever it was, Treasury objection was withdrawn. This garden is sited on what is known today as High Flyers' Hill, marked on John Norden's map of 1607 as Culver (pigeon) Hill.

Re-planting a rhododendron from Tower Court.

THE HYDRANGEA GARDEN

This lies on the very edge of the Valley Garden, and is described in Walk No.3 (see p.70, and note on p.177).

THE HEATHER AND DWARF CONIFER GARDEN

This garden was developed in 1954, the idea first suggested by the amount of wild heather and birch growing here, characteristic plants of heathland. In fact the site had been pitted as a result of gravel extraction prior to the First World War, but nature had resumed control. The present planting makes use of the undulations in the landscape and some of the natural flora, with the heathers punctuated by dwarf conifers and other small trees and shrubs.

Indigenous heathers here include **common heather** (*Calluna vulgaris*), which covers vast tracts of upland Britain and a couple of heaths: **Dorset heath** (*Erica ciliaris*), **bell-heather** (*E. cinerea*) and the **Cornish heath** (*E. vagans*). The exotic heathers come from the Iberian peninsula, Alpine Europe or one or two from South Africa. There are a few **tree heaths**: *Erica lusitanica*, *E. arborea* and *E. australis*, all Iberian heaths which can grow to over 1 metre in height.

Other ericaceous plants include
- *Gaultheria*, an evergreen flowering shrub, species of which are found in Asia and America and New Zealand;
- **bearberry** or *Arctostaphylos*, which is a low, creeping shrub used for ground cover;
- **bilberry/blueberry** and **cranberry** (*Vaccinium* species), which also have a creeping habit.

Other low cover includes grasses:
- **New Zealand Wind Grass** (*Stipa arundinacea*) which grows to about one metre in height.
- **The Spanish feather grass** (*Stipa gigantea*) which produces flowering spikes that can reach nearly two metres.
- Japanese *Miscanthus sinensis* 'Yakushima Dwarf' which grows to about 35cm.

Among the trees, look out for birches and sorbus trees
- the **river birch** (*Betula nigra*), is rare in Britain, so is worth looking at. It was first collected in eastern North America in 1736, probably by John Bartram. Its bark is pink-buff to orange, with long papery strips.
- the **Hupeh rowan** (*Sorbus hupehensis*), with its silvery grey-green leaves. It was first collected in western China in 1910.
- The **Arran whitebeam** (*S. arranensis*) which is found only on steep stream banks in the northern upland parts of Arran. It is among Britain's ten or so scarcest trees, approximately only 500 specimens surviving in their native habitat.

- **Tibetan whitebeam** (*S. wardii*), very rare in Britain. In fact it was first collected in Bhutan by Frank Kingdon-Ward (see p. 184), but is to be found in Burma, Bhutan and Tibet.

In addition there are blocks of **Scots pine** (*Pinus sylvestris*) and **North American Jack Pine** (*P. banksiana*), a rather rare pine for British gardens. This was first collected from its native habitat in eastern Canada in the eighteenth century, and named after Joseph Banks (1743-1820). Banks had made his name on the great exploratory voyage of HMS *Endeavour*, under Captain Cook, 1768-71. But he had already cut his teeth collecting plants in Newfoundland and Labrador. Banks went on to become the doyen of plant collecting in this great age of exploration, and it is he, principally, who established Kew's pre-eminence among the botanical gardens of Europe.

The dwarf and slow-growing conifers were developed in the late 1970s. The use of heathers and dwarf conifers in combination was a short-lived fashion at the time, and the intention here has been to maintain this example rather than lose it simply because such gardens have ceased to be fashionable.

THE PINETUM

This lies south west of the Heather Garden. You may wish to refer to a short general piece on conifers on p.172. Here, in the Pinetum, are specimens of various coniferous species including a **false cypress** (genus *Chamaecyparis*), **spruces** (genus *Picea*), **pines** (genus *Pinus*), and **silver firs** (genus *Abies*) so named because the undersides of the needles are silvery green, and hemlock (*Tsuga*).

- **Formosan or Taiwan cypress** (*Chamaecyparis formosensis*) was identified on Taiwan in 1910, where it can become of enormous size, with a girth of 20 metres. It remains rare and slow growing in Britain.

- **The Leyland cypress** (X *Cupressocyparis leylandii*), is so fast growing that it is a much favoured weapon in back garden disputes but here allowed uncontested free rein to be its unashamed and impressive self along the western crest of the Pinetum.
- **Brewer's weeping spruce** (*Picea brewerana*), with long pendulous branches and cones that are unusually thin for their length. It is rare in the wild and was only identified as a distinct species in the mountains of northern California in 1897.
- **Sikkim spruce** (*Picea spinulosa*) is rare in cultivation, but grows naturally in Sikkim and Bhutan where it was identified in the mid-nineteenth century by a gifted East India Company botanist and explorer, William Griffith.
- **Western yellow pine** (*Pinus ponderosa*) was first identified in Oregon and introduced by the great conifer collector, David Douglas, in 1827 (see p. 176). It can easily grow to 30 metres (there is even one at Powis Castle which is 41 metres tall). This tree was important in the development of the science of tree-ring dating in the early twentieth century.
- **Big cone pine** (*Pinus coulteri*) was found by David Douglas and his colleague Thomas Coulter in south west California in 1832. It lives up to its name with cones that can measure up to 35 x 20 cm and weigh up to 2kg. So if you see any cones, bear gravity in mind before walking under the branches. The tree itself can reach 30 metres in height.
- **Lace-bark pine** (*Pinus bungeana*) was first identified by European botanists in the wild in north-west China in 1846. It is a rarity in cultivation, so unless you have admired veteran examples in the Forbidden City in Beijing, you may wish to enjoy this one.
- **Chensien fir** (*Abies chensiensis*) was first identified by

European collectors in south west China in 1907.

- **Forrest's fir** (*Abies delavayi* var. *forrestii*) was found by George Forrest (see p. 179) in Yunnan and Sichuan, SW China, in 1910.
- **Giant fir** (*Abies grandis*) was first identified by David Douglas in 1830 in the Columbia river valley on the western slopes of the Rocky Mountains. Reporting to William Hooker in Britain, he exclaimed 'a forest of these trees is a spectacle too much for one man to see'. In the wild it has been known to grow to 100 metres, and there is one on Loch Fyne 63 metres tall.
- **Maries's fir** (*Abies mariesii*) on the west side of the valley is a rarity in Britain. It was identified by the English botanist Charles Maries in 1878. Maries trekked well over 400 miles from Tokyo northwards. He decided to explore Mt Hakkoda, spending a day trying to penetrate dense bamboo scrub to reach a new species of abies he could see, laden with cones. He returned to base empty handed and drenched to the skin after a round-trip of 34 miles. Undaunted he returned the next day, by a different route. He inadvertently but dangerously disturbed two black bears, but he got his seeds. Here one can admire his find with neither sweat nor peril.
- **Dawn redwood** (*Metasequoia glyptostroboides*), unlike other redwoods a deciduous tree, found in eastern Sichuan, China in 1941, here in a plantation abutting the Heather Garden. See p. 173 for its significance.
- **Western hemlock** (*Tsuga heterophylla*), a shapely tree, David Douglas found it widespread on the Columbia River in 1827 but inexplicably he never sent seed back to Britain, so it was not introduced here until 1851. But he recorded in his journal 'lofty snowy peaks in all directions. Contrasted with their dark shady bases densely covered with pine, the

deep rich hue of Pinus canadensis [the name he gave it] with its feathery cloudy branches quivering in the breeze.' No mountain here, but if you seek a mountainous context, there is a tree of about 50 metres height at Benmore, Argyll.

THE TOTEM POLE

There is much to say about this extraordinary object, erected here to mark British Columbia's centenary in 1958. The raw material is a 600 year-old Western red cedar (*Thuja plicata*) from Haida Gwai (Queen Charlotte Islands). Western red cedar was the timber favoured by the First Nations of coastal British Columbia for almost everything, including their timber lodges. David Douglas, with whose name you are fated to become familiar (see p.176), found it in 1826:

> 'This is a rapid growing and very graceful tree, in magnitude far exceeding any other species… Their form frequently exceeding one hundred and sixty feet in height and thirty-six feet in circumference six feet from the ground… No tree on the North West Coast is held in so much repute by the aborigines of the country… Their canoes… are made of the timber of this tree. The wood makes good shingles….'

Indeed, such sea-worthy canoes are still made. Their manufacture demands great skill, digging out the trunk and shaping it to an astonishing thinness and then widening it amidships by filling it with water and inserting red-hot rocks to make the water boil. Wooden jacks are then put across from one gunwale to the other to widen these apart. Such canoes remain artefacts of great beauty. More prosaically, the red cedar is still widely used for wall and roof shingles. It splits easily, making it very attractive to the North West Pacific coastal peoples before they had access to steel. If you are keen to see a good specimen

Wedding Party – Qagyuhl, Edward S. Curtis, The North American Indian, *vol. 10, The Kwakiutl,* (1915).

without travelling to British Columbia, there is western red cedar, 46 metres high, on Loch Fyne, Argyll. Much closer to hand, if you walk 300 metres up Canada Avenue, as it begins to curve to the right, there are a couple of very young specimens on your right. Opposite, on the left is a stand of several Wellingtonias (*Sequoiadendron giganteum*) followed by one Coast Redwood (*Sequoia sempervirens*). At full size, the Western Red Cedar acquires the same shaped trunk as these two species, the bole widening out, but also very fluted.

The various coastal First Nations produced totem poles or similar totemic carvings. Before the advent of Europeans up the Pacific coast, western red cedars were felled by placing red-hot rocks in cavities near the base of the trunk, or by splitting out the wood between two grooves cut around the trunk. Once felled, the carving was achieved with sharp stones and by splitting wood with antler or yew wedges. The carvings were coloured with pigments created by grinding various minerals and mixing

Masked dancers – Qagyuhl, with totem poles behind, Edward S. Curtis, The North American Indian, *vol. 10, The Kwakiutl, (1915).*

the powder with a binding agent, for example the glutinous part of salmon eggs. Once finished and erected, by use of ingenious rigging, the chief would hold a 'potlatch' (possibly the origin of the word 'potluck') a major and prolonged feast to demonstrate his prestige. The holding of prestigious feasts – just think of those state dinners up the road at the Castle – has been a fundamental gesture of human society from time immemorial.

The carvings usually represented a creature closely associated with an ancestor or deceased person, each creature carrying some well-known legend. This totem pole has been made by Chief Mungo Martin, a craftsman of the Kwakwaka'wakw (try saying that fast) nation, which inhabits the northern end of Vancouver Island and the mainland coast opposite. There are ten figures on this pole, each representing the mythical ancestor of one

VALLEY GARDENS

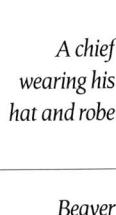

A chief wearing his hat and robe

Beaver

Old Man

Thunderbird

Sea Otter holding a seal

Raven (tail uppermost) his head between the fins of ...

... the Whale (which has a face for the blowhole)

A woman surrounded by Sisiutl, on whose head she is crouching

Halibut (tail uppermost) with a human within its body

Cedar Man

Notes:

Thunderbird is one of the most powerful of all spirits and a favourite among the Kwakwaka'wakw; thunder rolls from his beating wings, lightning flashes from his eyes, he preys on surfacing whales.

The Raven is associated with the Creation story.

Sisiutl, a triple headed sea monster, is associated with war and strength and is guardian of many houses.

particular kindred group. If you stand away uphill from the pole you will be able to identify each figure.

It is easy to react negatively to such an alien culture. If you remain unmoved, hang onto something that transcends the strangeness of totem poles and demands your respect and admiration. As with other peoples elsewhere (even the Gaels in Scotland), church and state went out of their way to suppress First Nation culture, proscribing the potlatch in the mid-nineteenth century and sending children away to mission schools to 'civilise' them. Coastal First Nation culture was reckoned to be in its death throes by the 1920s. Three generations later, in the 1950s, phoenix-like, there was a sudden flowering of First Nation cultural traditions and this renaissance continues to this day. In this totem pole, beyond these unfamiliar carvings, what you are really seeing is the triumph of the human spirit over cultural oppression. It should lift our spirits too, particularly since after centuries of trying to impose its values on others, the West still does not seem to have kicked the habit.

Plants of the Valley Gardens

AZALEAS

To most of us an azalea is an azalea, but not to any horticulturalist or botanist. A true azalea is a rare native plant, a dome-shaped shrub with small pink flowers to be found in rocky nooks above 350 metres in the Scottish highlands. To such botanists it is known as *Loiseleuria procumbens*. One will search in vain for an example at Windsor and they are rarely found in cultivation. What we think of and call azaleas are in reality rhododendrons. As early as 1796 Richard Salisbury, a botanist, confidently noted of the two:

> '….they agree minutely in habit, in florescence, filaments, anthers, grains of pollen adhering to each other by a glutinous thread, fruit, and seeds….'

The first such azalea to arrive in Britain was the happy outcome of science and religion working in tandem, and we have the Bishop of London to thank. Henry Compton had been appointed bishop in 1675 and wasted no time in developing the garden at Fulham Palace, his summer residence. He shrewdly appointed John Banister as missionary to Virginia which, like other New World possessions, fell effortlessly within the diocese of London. For he knew that while Banister was devoted to the faith he was in equal measure devoted to collecting, recording and drawing plant life. Compton waited and was duly rewarded. Among the many species he received from Banister was the 'Swamp Honeysuckle', *Rhododendron viscosum*, a hardy deciduous plant with long white tubular flowers and exotic scent. If you dislike smoking, you would have approved of Banister. He deplored the Virginia tobacco crop as a poor use of land that could produce food to eat and flax for clothing. Compton continued to receive American exotics, including the Sweet Gum (*Liquidambar styraciflua*), and the *Magnolia virginiana*. But in 1692 Compton received the melancholy news that Banister had become a martyr to horticulture. He had fallen over a cliff and perished while collecting plants.

We owe the next azalea imports to a remarkable Quaker partnership of two collectors who never met, Peter Collinson who maintained a small nursery in Peckham (and later at Mill Hill) and John Bartram living near New York. The fact that they were both Quakers was no coincidence. George Fox, the founder of the Society of Friends, had enjoined fellow Quakers to study 'the nature of herbs roots, plants and trees'. William Penn, whom Bartram had met in the New World, had likewise praised 'studying and following Nature, endeavouring to become a good naturalist'. So Bartram explored the swamps and rivers of the eastern seaboard, from Pennsylvania southwards to Florida. He sent Collinson many plants, among them more Swamp Honeysuckles and also the 'Pinxterbloom', *Rhododendron nudiflorum*, another deciduous azalea with abundant pink scented flowers, 'lavish without being ostentatious, graceful but not precious', a balance one suspects, almost too difficult to achieve. The name 'Pinxter' was New World dialect for Whitsun (presumably from '*Pfingsten*' the German term), when the plant was always in bloom. In the 1730s Bartram also sent home the acclaimed 'Flame Azalea', *Rhododendron calandulaceum*, which produces a striking orange blossom and is the parent of many hybrids. But the specimen was lost and another not obtained until 1806.

Wilson's Kurume Fifty   There are several hundred Kurume azalea varieties, being cultivars bred from locally occurring wild species by nurserymen on the southern island of Kyushu, Japan. Little known, even in Japan outside Kurume, they were made known to the Western world by a British collector, Ernest Wilson (1876-1930), who was born and bred in Gloucestershire. It was on his second visit to Japan in 1918 that he visited the leading Kurume nurseryman and selected fifty species which he considered the pick. These are the 'Wilson 50', now famous with all azalea lovers. About forty of these are here, a few proving insufficiently hardy.

Ernest Wilson (reproduced with kind permission of the Director and Board of Trustees, Royal Botanic Gardens, Kew).

Like George Forrest (see RHODODENDRONS, below), Ernest Wilson was noted for his dauntless courage and perseverance, principally in China. In 1903 he had been exploring a mountain in western Sichuan province. Near the summit he found himself facing more than one vertical cliff each of about 14 metres in height, with wooden ladders. What gave cause for concern, however, was that on either side there was a chasm at least 700 metres in depth:

> 'Up these [ladders] I carried my dog, never thinking of the descent. On returning he got frightened, and, though we had blindfolded him, he struggled much, and on one occasion his struggles all but upset my balance. I was heartily thankful when solid ground was reached. It requires all one's nerve

to mount a ladder, with no balustrade, fixed to a cliff 40 feet vertical and on either side a yawning abyss lost in the clouds.'

It was on a similar journey that 'through treading on some loose debris, I was only saved from being precipitated over a steep precipice by the presence of mind of a coolie who happened to be near me at the moment.'

Wilson mounted four expeditions to China. Later, in Formosa (today's Taiwan) in 1918, Wilson found himself plant collecting with a band of men described to him as 'reformed headhunters', with a couple of policemen to ensure no relapse on their part: 'Gathered around several fires were two score half-naked ex-head-hunters, armed with bows and arrows, long knives and guns....'

In 1910 Wilson had had a serious accident in Sichuan, breaking his leg in two places. He had to be carried for three days to reach Chengdu, where he could obtain medical assistance. It was three months before he could move on crutches, when he resumed his avid plant collecting. You cannot keep a good man down, but you can certainly make him limp. Thereafter, although the leg was re-set in America, Wilson's right leg remained significantly shorter than his left one. We owe a major debt to Wilson. Besides introducing the handkerchief tree (*Davidia involucrata*), he introduced some 1,200 species of trees and shrubs. If you love the Punch Bowl, remember him when next you have a glass in your hand.

CAMELLIAS

They may have no scent, but it is difficult to beat camellias in flower. They come from China and acquired their name from a Moravian, Georg Kamel (1661-1706), who became a Jesuit lay-brother and was sent to Manila in 1688, where he established a pharmacy to serve the poor. He probably never himself saw a camellia, but his Latinised name was given to the plant by Linnaeus, in honour of his published studies of plant specimens.

In fact, camellias were read about in Europe well before they were actually seen. Engelbert Kämpfer (1651-1715), a physician-botanist in the employ of the Dutch East India Company in Tokyo described 30 of the approximately 80 camellia species in 1712. Kämpfer certainly got around. He first travelled to Moscow, thence southwards to the Caspian, and on to Isfahan, Persepolis and Shiraz, before going to the coastal port of Bandar Abbas to proceed to Ceylon; from Ceylon he sailed to Java, and it was from there that he travelled to Japan, an impressive itinerary for the late seventeenth century.

Kämpfer suffered for science. On his visit to Tokyo not only was he closely guarded day and night, but he was also required to demonstrate to the Emperor and later to the Japanese nobility samples of European Culture. Thus he found himself in solo performance: jumping, singing, declaiming and dancing to replicate the extraordinary manners and customs of the Europeans to an astonished audience. He must have felt very silly and his audience totally perplexed. Thus, whatever the advances in science, they must have been achieved at huge cost to cross-cultural understanding.

Camellias were first introduced to Britain in c.1740 by Robert (8th Baron) Petre (1713-42), a Catholic noble who devoted his short life to botany and the pursuit of virtue. He struck up an informal partnership with Collinson in Peckham and Bartram in Pennsylvania. In 1739 he was cultivating bananas in his stove, or greenhouse, and when he died of smallpox aged only 29 in 1742, he had planted no fewer than 40,000 American trees on his estate: 'an anthology of the greatest collection of exotic trees ever naturalised' as the *Dictionary of National Biography* puts it.

If you wish to see the oldest camellias in the country, you will find them in the remarkably long conservatory in Chiswick House gardens, where ten survive from the 1820s. But you may feel such expeditions quite unnecessary. For we all keep camellia leaves in our kitchen and drink their infusion daily, *Camellia sinensis* making a very nice cup of tea.

CONIFERS

Conifers merit your attention. Britain itself has only three natives: the Scots pine (*Pinus sylvestris*), the yew (*Taxus baccata* L.) and the common juniper (*Juniperus communis*), essentially a shrub.

Yet conifers are the world's tallest (think of the Californian redwood or the Douglas fir) and longest-lived trees. Apart from the Californian bristlestone, which is probably the oldest, we have our own extremely ancient yew tree at Fortingal in Perthshire, anything between 3,000 to 5,000 years old, so it must have been alive in the days of Israel's King David. Today it is a shrivelled but living remnant, the victim of souvenir hunters. Yet in the late eighteenth century its trunk measured over 17 metres in circumference.

Conifers appeared nearly 300 million years ago, long before the first dinosaurs. Today we have only a few relicts from the days when a multiplicity of conifers flourished, belonging to eight families containing a total of 70 genera, most of which now have five or fewer species apiece, approximately 360 species in all. The principal reason for conifer decline is that during the past 100 million years they have been increasingly challenged by a more sophisticated kind of plant, one that flowers (angiosperms). A secondary reason is that over the past 150 years conifers have been the victim of an unprecedented amount of logging that has destroyed great swathes of coniferous forest, notably in North America.

Despite their retreat, conifers can still see off most tree angiosperms in extreme conditions, in cold, heat or aridity (*pace* cacti). The cones which conifers produce are always male or female, never hermaphrodite (unlike so many angiosperms). Many conifers bear both male and female cones on the same tree, although some do not.

There are plenty of conifers in the south-eastern section of Windsor Great Park, particularly in the Valley Gardens, where many exotics have been planted. Do not forget the Dwarf and Slow Growing Conifer Collection in the Heather Garden.

Conifers to look out for:

Redwoods (part of the Taxodiaceae family) have three surviving genera:
- the coastal redwood (*Sequoia*)
- the giant sequoia (*Sequoiadendron*)
- the dawn redwood (*Metasequoia*)

Of the genus *Sequoia* the one surviving species is the coastal redwood (*Sequoia sempervirens*). There are a number of specimens in the Valley Gardens although they truly prefer life on the Pacific coast, where they absorb one third of their water intake from the ocean mists that condense on its foliage.

Of the genus *Sequoiadendron* only the giant sequoia or Wellingtonia (*S. giganteum*) survives, naturally on the western slopes of the Sierra Nevada of California. It was introduced to Britain 1853. Several examples are growing in the Valley Gardens

As for the last of these genera, only one species had survived, the dawn redwood species (*Metasequoia glyptostroboides*). Until 1941 it was only known as a fossil, which had flourished between 180 and 130 million years ago. That year a living cluster of about 25 specimens was found in south-west China. Introduced to Britain in 1948, it has since then been anxiously propagated. Where once they were rare, indeed assumed extinct, now they are common. But that is no reason for not admiring the specimens here, on the fringe of the Heather Garden and head of the Pinetum. Like the Ginkgo tree, it is a relic of Mesozoic times, flourishing between 180 and 130 million years ago).

Cedars (*Cedrus*) are a group of four species. The first to arrive in Britain was the **cedar of Lebanon** (1638). There are two other Mediterranean species. The **Cyprus ceda**r (*Cedrus brevifolia*) was identified following Britain's shabby acquisition of the island in 1878, but remains rare in Britain. **The Atlantic** (or Atlas) **cedar** (*Cedrus atlantica*), native to Algeria and Morocco, arrived in Britain in 1841. It is most often seen in Britain in its variety 'Glauca', with highly attractive blue-grey foliage. Finally, from the Himalayas, but closely related to the others, is the **Deodar cedar** (*Cedrus deodara*) introduced by Joseph Hooker in 1831. Cedars all have a spreading habit. This is no accident. They get plenty of sunlight in the low latitiudes where they are found. The more extreme the latitude, the more steeply conical conifers tend to be, desperately seeking to catch horizontal winter sunlight.

Crudely speaking one may identify the three principal cedar species by looking at the young tips of the branches of mature trees: Atlantic *ascend*, Lebanon are *level* and Deodar *descend*. But it is still easy to make mistakes, particularly with younger specimens. There are examples of each in the Valley Gardens, particularly Lebanon and Deodar cedars, for example close to the Obelisk and also near the Gardens car park.

Pines (*Pinus*) are almost all adapted to poor soil. Several of the 109 species grow in the Valley and Savill gardens. One of the least common is the **Montezuma pine** (*Pinus montezumae*) which has a uniquely broad dome of large blue-grey upswept tufts of unusually long needles. The broad dome, of course, betrays its latitude, one with plenty of overhead sun. In its native Mexico it can reach a height of 20 metres. If you wish to see it, walk up Canadian Avenue and turn left near the top, where you pass a short row of tall Wellingtonias. It is about 100 metres into the lawn area of 'Elcocks'.

Larches (*Larix*) 11 species. Unlike most conifers, larches are deciduous, a relative of the cedar.

Firs (*Abies*) 48 species, unlike most conifers, firs prefer richer soils but most species are content to endure extreme cold. *Abies grandis* on the west coast of British Columbia can reach almost 90 metres in height. There are examples in the Pinetum. Examples of the **noble fir** (*A. procera*), from N.W. America set off the azaleas of the Punch Bowl very effectively.

Spruces (*Picea*) 34 species, including the archetypal **Christmas tree**. They grow in northern regions around the world. There are plenty here.

Hemlocks (*Tsuga*) 9 species, one of several genera confined to Asia and North America, indicating that the two continents were once joined. The **western hemlock** (*Tsuga heterophylla*) may be found in the Pinetum, and the **eastern hemlock** (*Tsuga Canadensis*), a slow-growing tsuga, cultivars of which can be found in the Heather Garden.

Pseudotsuga (4 species), also straddles the Bering Straits. The most famous, perhaps, is the **Douglas fir** (*P. menziesii*) which grows along the western seaboard of North America. It is among the largest trees of all, the largest tree on record was 127 metres high, outstripping even coastal redwoods. The Douglas fir flagpole in Kew Gardens is a mere whippersnapper, at 60 metres. Smaller Douglas firs grow here in the Valley Gardens.

The species was one of very many collected by David Douglas (1799-1834) on the three hair-raising expeditions he made to North America. Douglas was the son of a stonemason at Scone in Perthshire. On his expeditions, Douglas frequently found himself in desperate straits, from hunger, exposure or the hostility of Native Americans. He always travelled light, carrying his plant specimens on his back. His clothes list for a 19-week expedition into the mountains, where the temperature often fell below freezing, was 'two shirts, two handkerchiefs, blanket and cloak and one pair of shoes but no stockings'. You will not therefore be surprised that having spent a night soaked to the skin and in freezing cold, he confided to his journal 'If I had any zeal, for once and the first time it began to cool.' More than once he found himself without food, having to survive on rats, berries and roots, or bartering his handkerchiefs or clothes buttons with Native Americans in return for meat. Nothing daunted him, but he was sometimes profoundly lonely, admitting on one foray that he was 'haunted continually by the thought that our people, who were daily expected from the coast, would have arrived and brought my letters'. And when he finally met a party carrying his mail, he wrote 'I am not ashamed to say I rose from my mat four different times during the night to read my letters; in fact, before morning I might say I had them by heart – my eyes never closed'. Douglas fell down ravines, saw off hostile Native Americans, lost his collections while swimming across or canoeing down rivers (it happened at least twice), nearly got lost when heavy snowfall hid the blazes on tree trunks, and spent many nights numb and shaking with wet, cold and wind. 'On such occasions,' he remarked as if confessing to a weakness, 'I am very liable to become fretful.' He reported the discovery of so many new species of conifer that he wrote to William Hooker, yet to become the director at Kew, 'you will begin to think I manufacture Pines at my pleasure'. Reckless to the end, Douglas died aged only 35 when, peering into a pit trap in Hawaii, the edge apparently collapsed beneath his weight and he was gored to death by the trapped wild cow below.

Like most great men, Douglas had a streak of eccentricity. He occasionally sported a suit of Royal Stuart tartan, hardly one of the quieter hues. Needless to say, it gave rise to open-mouthed wonder, more among white settlers than Native Americans, who were probably up for anything. Douglas had a well-earned reputation for impatience and recklessness, yet whatever his failings, he remains a colossus among collectors, explorers and geographers.

HYDRANGEAS

Hydrangeas hale from North America and also the Far East. The first hydrangea (*H. arborescens*) reached Britain in 1736, having been collected by the tireless John Bartram on the eastern seaboard of north America and duly despatched to his colleague Collinson in London, who persuaded it to flower. Its popular relative, *H. arborescens grandiflora* was found in Pennsylvania only c.1900. Both are white. Those from the Far East were introduced to Europe principally through the agency of the Dutch East India Company from the closing years of the eighteenth century through until c.1840. The common hydrangea or hortensis (*H. macrophylla*) was introduced by an English collector, Charles Maries, as a result of his collecting in Japan in 1877. It is well known for its propensity to turn pink on anything but acid soil with aluminium trace elements. There are also *H. villosa*, which produces pale purple flowers and *H. sargentiana*, with rose-lilac flowers, both introduced from China.

MAGNOLIAS

Incontestably among the most beautiful flowering trees, they are, in fact, probably one of the closest to the very first primitive angiosperms, or flower bearing plants. Magnolia flowers, like water lilies, are very simple in composition compared with later developments. They grow naturally in the Americas and in southeast Asia. The first introductions from 1736 onwards were found in the south-eastern part of North America. John Bartram (see AZALEAS) was, of course, one of the first on the scene. At first they were called Laurel-Tulip trees, but then renamed in honour of a Montpellier horticulturist, Pierre Magnol (1638-1715), who was the intellectual father of the structure and theory of Linnaeus' method of plant nomenclature. The Valley Gardens comprise a National Collection of magnolias, with over 310 species and cultivars, which divide into two broad categories, those that are 'precocious', i.e. flowering before they come into leaf, and those that are not.

RHODODENDRONS

It is easy to think that the collection of plants from distant places has fundamentally been a gentle, uncontroversial activity. That, doubtless, has been implicit in the intention but certainly not always the experience. There has always been an element of risk.

As a young collector, Joseph Hooker landed at Calcutta in 1848 and proceeded to Sikkim, which was still largely unexplored. He was an unwelcome guest, for the raja's chief minister was rightly suspicious of his activities, particularly his mapping of the landscape. Hooker had been prohibited from crossing Sikkim's northern border into Tibet and when he deliberately disobeyed, the chief minister had him thrown into prison. It was an unwise move against the subject of the principal world power. Britain threatened Sikkim with invasion, Hooker was released and Britain decided to reward itself for the general inconvenience with the confiscation of some of Sikkim's lands. Invasion, war and land expropriations are not what one normally thinks of when contemplating a botanising expedition. But this was Britain almost at the height of its imperial power (and global misbehaviour).

When Hooker went on to Nepal he very wisely arranged for an escort of Gurkhas, even today the best possible guarantee against unwarranted interference. He collected about 7,000 plant species, including 25 entirely new rhododendrons, thereby increasing the known repertoire by 50 per cent. In fact he made his name with the rhododendrons he discovered, and his *Rhododendrons of the Sikkim-Himalaya* (1849-51) played a major part in the rhododendron craze that ensued. It was his proud father, William Hooker, director at Kew, who observed: 'Perhaps with the exception of the Rose, the queen of flowers, no plants have excited more interest throughout Europe than the several species of *Rhododendron*.' Joseph in due course succeeded his father as director at Kew.

Plant collecting has sometimes demanded huge physical courage and determination, even in the twentieth century. Here is a tale to stop you in your tracks (and once you have read it you will forgive me for its length). One of the most colourful collectors of rhododendron species was George Forrest. Born in Falkirk in 1873, he first took a job as a shop assistant in a local pharmacy. After a brief and unsuccessful plant-collecting foray to Australia

George Forrest freshly arrived from Britain, at the China Inland Mission, Dali, Yunnan.

and South Africa, he took a post in the Edinburgh Botanic Garden in 1902. A couple of years later he was commissioned by a private naturalist to collect plants for him in western China, and it was here that Forrest worked until his death in 1932. In all he made seven major collecting trips, after a first unsuccessful foray that would have put most of us off collecting abroad for life.

By ill-fortune, this first venture in 1904-5 coincided with the notoriously disgraceful Younghusband military expedition into Tibet, which provoked a Tibetan rising with the avowed aim of killing all foreigners that fell into their hands. The Tibetans carried swords, poisoned arrows and were accompanied by mastiffs. Already in southern Tibet, Forrest got word of this rising while staying with French missionaries. Forrest wished to flee immediately but, fatally, the missionaries dallied and he felt a duty to his hosts. They were cut off on their way out. Forrest's letter to his previous employer is still at the Royal Botanic Garden, Edinburgh and you will share my gratitude that I have been allowed to reproduce excerpts here:

> 'In a short time I saw what I expected, a band of 40 to 50 men come tearing along the ridge at full speed.... Immediately all was confusion, and from that moment forward, it was every

man for himself…. I chose to go down the stream towards the
Mekong, which lay about 2 miles to the east. That frightful
race I shall never forget, and how I escaped death I cannot say.
The path was in most places formed of brackets in the faces
of the cliffs, scores of feet above the stream which thundered
beneath. At those parts it consisted merely of two eight inch
logs slippery and rotten from continual moisture and spray. Yet
over these I went racing as if I had been on an ordinary good
road. Towards the end of the valley…. the path took a sharp
bend, and as I turned round this I came face to face with seven
lamas and Tibetan soldiers, all armed to the teeth. They …
instantly spotted me and gave chase…. I turned and fled in the
direction I had come, then, before they had reached the corner,
I made a jump into the scrub on the stream side of the path….'

For eight days Forrest was relentlessly hunted, hiding during daylight hours and only moving by night along the banks of the Mekong, which was in flood.

'The second evening I went back on my old track a short
distance and discovered that my pursuers had been following
me by the marks made by my boots. These I immediately
discarded, buried, then descended to the stream, entered the
water and waded up west for nearly a mile, taking the utmost
care when I got out to leave no track. To this, I think, I owe
my escape…. Several times I saw detached bodies of lamas….
Once whilst lying asleep behind a log in the bed of a stream,
I was awakened by a sound of laughing and talking, and
on looking up I discovered about thirty of them in the act of
crossing the steam about fifty yards above my hiding place. It
was a very near squeak.'

Forrest spent much of his time hiding in the rhododendron thickets from which he would, in quieter circumstances, have been collecting seed samples.

Back in Dali, George Forrest shortly after his dramatic escape, much leaner and still dressed in the disguise that helped secure his survival.

'The flowers I saw were really magnificent, in fact, so fine were they, that I have decided to run the risk of going back next year if Mr Bulley gives his consent to the arrangement. There are several species of Meconopsis, all of them surpassingly lovely.... ditto rhododendrons, many of which I had never seen before.'

What a player.

'By the end of eight days I must have presented a most hideous spectacle, clothes hanging in rags, and covered in mud, almost minus breeches, face and hands scarred and scratched with fighting my way through scrub in the dark, feet ditto, and swollen almost beyond semblance of feet, shaggy black beard and moustache, and, I have no doubt, a most terrified, hungry and hunted expression on my countenance.'

Forrest had begun to hallucinate and realised he could go without food no longer. So he took the risk of entering a small hamlet. The headman proved friendly. He hid and fed Forrest, clothed him in Chinese garb and then passed him from one friendly headman to another. It was at this stage that Forrest suffered another disaster, for he trod on a bamboo spike hidden on the track, an anti-poaching device laid by local farmers. This spike passed straight through his foot, projecting a couple of inches. It is difficult to think of such things without wincing, but

Forrest's team of plant collectors. On the left is Lao Chao, who accompanied Forrest on all his subsequent expeditions. Forrest only shot for the pot, but the guns may have been for defence against wild animals also. Note the press for plant specimens in the foreground.

Forrest omitted this incident from his letter, a detail perhaps too insignificant for this hard man to recount. By the time he reached safety he had been marching for three weeks and was in a terrible state. He was less concerned by his physical condition than by the loss of his field-notes, photographs and specimens of more than 2,000 different plants and seeds of 80 species.

It was on the basis of this thorough education in the unpredictability of life that Forrest returned in 1910 to the same region of the upper Mekong and the Sino-Burmese border, an area that was to be the focus of, in all, seven highly fruitful expeditions. We owe many species of rhododendron and camellia to his work. He died of a heart attack very suddenly aged 59, while relaxing at the end of his final expedition, the price, one suspects, of an excess of early excitement. He discovered over 300 rhododendron species, and, like Ernest Wilson and David Douglas, deserves a toast next time you have a glass in your hand. And remember: plant collecting is not for cissies.

Another great collector of rhododendrons and other flora in eastern Asia was Frank Kingdon-Ward (1885-1958). Kingdon-Ward spent his childhood a stone's throw away, in Englefield Green and in his retirement very appropriately was consulted regarding the siting of various rhododendron species in the Valley Gardens.

Rhododendron is, of course, the predominant genus in the Valley Gardens. The Species Collection comprises only wild species, with over 800 examples, spread out over Breakheart Hill and High Flyers Hill. Hybrids may be found, along with wild species, in the Main Valley.

The Political Landscape

It may seem surprising to call any landscape 'political', but undoubtedly this is how one should describe the process of evolution from forest to hunting park, thence to landscaped park and gardens. The landscape and its uses reflect a progression from the near absolute powers of medieval monarchy to today's democracy within a constitutional monarchy.

WINDSOR FOREST

"No Forest, of them all, so fit as she doth stand,
When Princes, for their sportes, her pleasure will command,
No wood-nymph as herselfe such troupes hath ever seene,
Nor can such quarries boast as have in Windsor beene.
Nor any ever had so many solemne dayes;
So brave assemblies view'd, nor took so rich assaies."
                    Michael Drayton, *Polyolbion*, 1613.

Windsor Great Park represents only a small portion of the medieval Windsor Forest, once a very large tract of land. At the beginning of the seventeenth century this forest still stretched as far west as the present A33 running southwards from Reading, and as far south as Guildford and the Hog's Back, and with a circumference of approximately 200 kilometres (120 miles).

One might unsuspectingly think that forest was by definition woodland but 'forest' was a legal term indicating a tract of land in which game could be hunted. Whether it was wooded or not was incidental, except for the usefulness of wooded areas in which game could shelter. Forest was a place of game, notably deer, not necessarily of trees.

By 1066 England was already a denuded landscape (see p. 209). Forests had plenty of open areas, principally ones of wood pasture, a landscape of pasture with both timber and pollard (see p. 210) trees. There would also have been tracts of heathland. Except for small and specific enclosed areas, there would be no fencing or hedging, in order not to impede the chase.

Several forests in England predated the Norman invasion, and Windsor Forest was probably one of them. It was one of only five forests described in the Domesday Survey of 1088. Nevertheless, the idea of forest rapidly became identified with the Normans. William I and his successors were passionate hunters and expanded the tracts designated as forest and subject to Forest Law, outside the reach of the law of either Church or State. At its peak perhaps one third of England was designated forest. For the next five centuries hunting remained a royal obsession. Kings hunted both red and fallow deer, the latter having been re-introduced by the Normans from the Levant. They knew that fallow deer were good meat producers on poor soil. The Normans also hunted virtually any other creatures one cares to name: badgers, foxes, hares, pigeons and also two other Norman imports, rabbits and partridges. Wolves and wildcat were found and hunted to extinction in Windsor Forest. In 1617 James I hunted wild boar here, which must have been for more or less the last time, since wild boar were effectively extinct in England by 1700.

Hunting was much more than a pastime. It was, in Simon Schama's words, 'the most significant blood ritual through which status and honour were established.... an arena in which families and members of families competed for proximity to the monarch'. In peacetime hunting provided the essential apprenticeship for knightly horsemanship, just as it had done in the Ancient World and just as foxhunting has done more recently. As early as the age of eight, for example, the future king, Edward I (1239-1307), had been granted permission to hunt in Windsor Forest, a suitable preparation for his later career, waging war on the Saracens, the French, the Welsh and the Scots.

Specific draconian laws were introduced by the Normans to deter ordinary mortals from any interference in these forests. Forest officers were charged with the protection of 'the vert and the venison', essentially all valuable plant product, be it grazing, underwood or timber, and any form of meat. In theory anyone caught stealing, killing or maiming game, principally deer, boar or hare, might be liable to extreme punishment. Those still living in the forest were required to 'law' any dog they might own, which meant amputation of the three claws of the fore paws, so that they were unable to attack game. Forest tenants were allowed to graze a few domestic animals but this right was very strictly controlled.

Inevitably such laws gave rise to enormous resentment. There must have been great *schadenfreude* among the subject Saxons at the death of William II (Rufus), shot through the eye by an arrow while hunting in 1100. He may have been the most notable fatality in a notoriously dangerous sport, but there were others. His brother, Richard, was also killed hunting in the New Forest, as was his nephew, another Richard. Thus the Conqueror lost two sons and a grandson. 'Poetic justice', Saxon peasants must have thought. William's successor, his brother, Henry I (1100-1137), was supposedly less brutal, but for those caught violating forest law he still favoured punishments such as blinding, castration or execution.

Many myths grew up about Norman brutality, but these were inevitably prone to exaggeration, partly because this was a hated foreign-speaking warrior caste lording it over a subject people. Major expulsions of peasants never actually took place, principally because the forests were located on the least productive land with marshy or acidic soils, as here.

The resentment felt among the peasantry was shared by a growing number of barons, yeomen and freemen. Many, even nobles, were falsely accused of forest offences, simply as a revenue-raising or land-grabbing gambit. By 1200 forests were a serious political issue. It was the nobility, not the peasantry, who rebelled against John. They forced him to sign Magna Carta, just down the road at Runnymede, in 1215 and compelled his successor, Henry III, to concede a Forest Charter in 1217, returning land afforested by Henry II and his sons, Richard I and John, in the preceding half century, to their previous owners. Your home may well be on old forest land, for Henry II had extended Windsor Forest as far as Hungerford in the west and well into Buckinghamshire, Middlesex and Hampshire.

Henry I's policy of mutilation or execution for killing game had probably already fallen into abeyance but the new Forest Charter explicitly prohibited such barbarities. From 1217 one could only be fined, or imprisoned for a year and a day if unable to pay the fine. 'Trespassers against the venison' were frequently imprisoned. Those caught in Windsor Forest often found themselves incarcerated in the castle. Indeed, they were probably the castle's principal prisoners.

The 'stint' (the individual tenant's quota whether of domestic animals grazing in specific areas of the forest or of underwood and fodder) continued to be maintained, as was the lawing of dogs. Grazing rights, particularly the right to allow pigs to graze for acorns in the forest, known as 'pannage', were now allowed by right to all free men, but were also strictly rationed. Those exceeding their stint would be fined.

By the thirteenth century, however, libertarian myths began to grow, reflecting a number of truths and half-truths about the forest: that it had once been the 'waste' enjoyed by the community, as had been partly true in Anglo-Saxon times, and that it was a haven for freedom-loving souls. 'The greenwood of Old England' excited fantasies of freeborn, independent-minded Englishmen living beyond the reach of the tyrannies that existed beyond the forest, and one automatically thinks of heroic Saxon resisters, like Hereward the Wake.

In reality, however, the forest tracts were a haven for brigands. By 1230 Windsor Forest was notorious for the large number of poachers and fugitives, armed with bow and arrow, men who might well kill or wound one of the Crown foresters. 'Never ask where the meat comes from' was a common saying. That the forest was a haven for fugitives from Norman law melded with the sense of Saxon dispossession, often of small landholders, to produce the mythical Robin Hood, a wronged yeoman and his merry men standing up against the tyrannies of Church and State. The first printed editions of *Lytell Geste of Robyn Hode* appeared over two centuries later, in the second half of the fifteenth century, at first the stuff of ballads sung in manor houses, but eventually the subject matter of popular song in the village inn. In his rebellion against officers of both government and the church, Robin Hood also reflected the true meaning of the original Latin word for forest, *foris*, meaning 'outside', in this context signifying outside the interference of Church and State rather than beyond settled agricultural areas. The royal forests were subject to their own laws, always something apart. Robin Hood is England's most famous mythical forest hero, righting a wronged world. Yet here, in Windsor Forest, there is a similar legend, one that is historically untrue but which does concern a real but wronged person, Fulk Fitzwarine (see p. 199).

It was principally the cost of war between the mid-eleventh and late thirteenth centuries that changed the forest: Henry II's wars to safeguard his territories in France; Richard's war against the

Saracens in the Holy Land; Henry III's wars against his barons and Edward I's wars against the Welsh and Scots. These wars all put great strains on the exchequer and as a result forest tracts came under pressure to yield profit. By 1300, too, the population had grown rapidly, with increasing demand for productive land. As a consequence, the Crown and those few magnates who also held forestlands began to rent out tracts for profit, allowing open pasture or arable to be cut, or 'assarted', from the forest.

Nevertheless, the term 'Windsor Forest' continued to apply to large tracts of land down the centuries. Charles I re-introduced Forest Law although it had lain dormant for generations. Predictably this provoked massive local resentment. Perhaps sensing the coming collapse of royal authority, bands of locals broke through the fences surrounding the Great Park to access 'the venison and the vert' as they had become accustomed to do as of right. That was in April-May 1642. Three months later civil war broke out. Never again was there any serious attempt to re-introduce the severe strictures of Forest Law.

By 1806, the extent of Windsor Forest had been reduced by about half since the Middle Ages, but still had a circumference of roughly 100 kilometres, or 56 miles. Steps were taken by acts of parliament over the following decade or so for piecemeal disafforestation.

Windsor Forest enjoyed an enduring and unsavoury reputation for banditry. By customary law, the local community was responsible for ensuring safety on its roads, and was liable to compensate for highway robbery. It is an indication of the extent of the problem that in the late sixteenth century an Act of Parliament provided exceptional relief for the inhabitants of the Sunninghill district from this liability. A cluster of eight village or hamlets had already been reduced to penury in paying £255 for robberies committed in their area, a sum equivalent to over

£40,000 in today's money, inflicted on an essentially subsistence population. In the mid-seventeenth century Windsor Forest was a favoured territory for the notoriously expert shot and swordsman, Claude Duval, before he was captured and hanged. In 1723 a gang of 40 men, 'the Waltham Blacks', involved in deer stealing, intimidation, theft and murder, were finally suppressed. Four of the gang, two of whom were captured in Cranbourne (see Walk No. 1) were hanged and their corpses then hung from local gibbets as a deterrent. These gibbets were metal or chain frames in which the body slowly decayed over the years, pecked by birds, the skin progressively shrivelled away from the bone, the source of many a childhood nightmare. In fact a principal motive for the piecemeal disafforestation of major parts of Windsor Forest was to stamp out brigandage. By converting tracts of the Forest to pasture, meadow, arable and to enclosed commons, the areas where local miscreants could hide were greatly reduced. More importantly, perhaps, they were now subject to common law. Some of the commons within the forest, for example, were allotted to private owners, most notably the Crown.

However, Windsor Forest as a coherent entity was never formally disafforested. Everything happened piecemeal. Furthermore, in confirmation of a continuing regard for this landscape, the Crown Lands Act of 1961 required that the Windsor estate should be maintained so as to retain the character of 'a royal park and forest'. Do not think this is simply another example of heritage mania. Windsor Great Park and areas still marked as 'Windsor Forest' on the map are managed with exceptional eco-sensitivity, and boast more species of invertebrate, some unique to the area, than any other location in Britain.

DEER PARKS

Deer parks were essentially the creation of Norman kings and barons. Anyone holding enough land could create a livestock park. A substantial number were located in the poor agricultural areas where the Surrey, Berkshire and Middlesex borders meet.

The sudden increase in the number of deer parks from the late twelfth century may have been in response to the introduction of fallow deer earlier that century. They proved much easier to keep in a confined space than red deer. That there were once many such parks, employing many staff, cannot be doubted. Think how common a surname 'Parker' is.

No one knows quite how old the Great Park actually is. Old Windsor had been a fortified site with a royal residence in Saxon times. It possessed an enclosure, which may have been a game park. Certainly by 1130 there are indications that a park had been established here. In the 1240s, during the reign of Henry III, a substantial moated manor house was built within a pale towards the south end of the present Great Park. The site is now an island on the north side of Virginia Water, adjacent to the confluence with Johnson's Pond. While it is known that Henry and his family used this Manor Lodge as their principal abode while hunting, we do not know whether there was a previous building there, or how long this piece of the forest may have been set aside as a hunting park. But it represents the documented start of the Great Park, approximately within the boundaries that we know today. On the north-western, northern and north-eastern sides of the Great Park, the remains of the thirteenth or fourteenth century pale, unmistakable banks, may still easily be found. By 1270 all the wild cattle inside the designated area had been rounded up and sold off, and the park re-stocked with fallow deer from Chute Forest on the Hampshire-Wiltshire border. Transporting these deer must have been a major undertaking, presumably all brought here overland.

During this period another moated lodge and park, Wychmere, was incorporated into the park, in 1359. This stood very close to Old Windsor, and is now known as Bear's Rails. Other parks with moated lodges lay nearby. Moat Park, also probably created sometime between 1250 and 1350, was not annexed until the seventeenth century, so traces of its own boundary pales survive. Finally, Tile Place Manor, adjacent to Bear's Rails but to the north, was not incorporated into the Crown Estate until the nineteenth century, by which time it had long been a farm.

The Great Park was the scene of major equestrian gatherings, ones of great political and military significance. Of these, the tournament was central and pre-eminent. By the end of the Middle Ages this type of individual combat had become greatly formalised with rules to epitomise the idea of chivalry, romantically illustrated in Scott's *Ivanhoe*. Yet in the early Middle Ages tournaments frequently descended into unseemly affrays between rival gangs of retainers. The idea of individual combat, not to kill but to secure the submission of one's opponent, was irresistible to the warrior caste, for it embodied the knightly obsession with valour. It was still extremely dangerous, even when the weapons used were specifically designed for sport rather than for war. Such was the attraction of the tournament that the more obsessed knights would even desert a military campaign to participate. Two or three knights, for example, absconded from the English army in Scotland in order to participate in a tournament at Byfleet in Surrey, 400 miles away. Such desertion tended to attract punishment and admiration in equal measure, for most English kings were also addicted to the tourney. Edward I was among the keenest. He had cut his teeth in the lists at the age of sixteen and never looked back. In

July 1278, he held a major tournament in the Great Park, attended by some 38 nobles and knights, some of whom had previously accompanied him on crusade to the Holy Land, among them Roger of Trumpington.

'Round Tables' were elaborated forms of tournament, which might extend over a fortnight. They involved pageant, feasting and individual combat. Ladies attended, thus ensuring singing and dancing after the day's more dangerous sport in the lists had ended. These were celebrations of chivalry, but they were more. Some were propaganda events replete with Arthurian overtones. For Edward I the assertion may have been his legitimacy as lord over the other Britons of the Arthurian kingdom: the Welsh and the Scots. For his grandson, Edward III, the target was the French, for the Arthurian legend implied the invincibility of the band of chivalric brothers gathered around the Table, over all comers.

Roger of Trumpington, 1289, Trumpington Church, near Cambridge.

The most famous of these Round Tables occurred here in the Great Park in 1344. Indeed, Edward III had planned a round table for the occasion, to be housed in a round house, 200 feet in diameter, at Windsor. In part Edward was asserting, like his grandfather, the cult of English kingship. Yet he was also playing a political game. His short-lived Order of the Round Table, inaugurated at this event, was open to 300 knights of any nationality who passed muster in the lists. In reality the new order seems to have been an élite recruiting tool against the French, to whom this natty wheeze came as an unwelcome indication of Edward's military cunning, which complimented his martial skills so ably demonstrated on the battlefield of Crécy two years later. But the Round Table was also useful for foreign magnates who were engaged in their own conflicts. They, too, came to the Great Park in 1344 to talent-spot and recruit. Their modern equivalents, of course, attend football matches. Four years later, in 1348, the much smaller Order of the Garter was inaugurated at Windsor, after another chivalric event in the Great Park. From then on, the Order of the Garter was considered the true descendant of the Arthurian Round Table, a potent tool in myth-making about the established order. As one walks this landscape, therefore, one cannot possibly pretend it is not resonantly political.

The principal characteristic of all parks and warrens is that they were enclosed securely, always to prevent the egress of livestock back into the forest or countryside. This was usually achieved at great expense by the construction of a bank with a pale, usually cleft oak staves driven into the bank, and a ditch on the inside. The staves would be reinforced with horizontal rails to prevent a gap appearing, the term 'rails' being another indicator of an erstwhile livestock park. The ditch was to inhibit the livestock from attempting to leap the pale. Quite a few were designed to allow the ingress of livestock, via a 'deer leap' to which wild animals might be driven. It would be composed of a ramp on the outside; a gap in the pale and a drop on the inside to prevent escape, except into the park. Parks emphasised, even more than forest, strong Norman ideas about private property distinct from their more community-minded Saxon predecessors.

Increasingly, however, deer parks became venison farms, and by the end of the fifteenth century they became fashionable 'amenities' for the nobility. Yet hunting enjoyed a revival in the reign of Henry VIII, himself a passionate hunter, as was his daughter, Elizabeth, and as were the first two Stuart kings.

Deer parks were a particularly English fashion. In 1549 a Frenchman surmised that there were as many deer in England as people in France. A much-travelled contemporary reckoned that England probably had as many deer parks as the rest of Europe put together. Queen Elizabeth had no fewer than 200 deer parks of her own, less a fashion and more an obsession, one might say.

We know James was a hunting obsessive, for only three days after the unmasking of the Gunpowder Plot, with much of England in uproar, James insisted on hunting in the deer park he had created adjacent to Richmond Palace, to the consternation of his security chiefs. In our present climate of anti-terror precautions, his insouciance and *sangfroid* are refreshing. One gets an impression of James I's routine from the report:

> 'Sometimes he comes to Counsell, butt most tyme he spendes in Fields and Parkes and Chases, chasinge away idleness by violent exercise and early rysinge.'

Charles I found his father's park too small and enclosed a new park on the high ground above the palace, which survives to this day as Richmond Park.

By the beginning of the seventeenth we know from Norden's map that the Great Park was divided into three discrete parks, from south to north: the Manor Walk, the largest one covering the whole of the southern landscape of the park up to a line very roughly from just south of Leiper Pond across to the present Savill Gardens; the Middle Walk, which ran northwards to an approximate line from Forest Gate eastwards to just south of Bishopsgate; finally the northern and smallest section was called the Lower Walk. Norden marks the Middle and Lower Walks as containing deer, but not the Manor Walk. Indeed, Norden's survey states

> 'there is in Manor Walk a game of coines [coneys, i.e. rabbits] the burroughs whereof extend themselves scatteringly over a great parte of the said walke, which said ground wee find to be stocked with Conies.'

So it is not surprising that it was to the Manor Park that Charles I came to hunt rabbits and squirrels. The abundance of rabbit holes would have rendered the landscape dangerous for mounted hunting. Deer hunting probably took place, as Norden's map implies in the Middle and Lower Walks.

With the execution of Charles and the establishment of Cromwell as Lord Protector, the deer parks were plundered by ex-soldiers and local people, and the palings taken for firewood. Charles II returned the landscape to parkland and began restocking it with deer. John Evelyn records in his diary for August 1670:

> 'The King passed most of his time hunting the stag, &c Walking in the Parke which he was now also planting with rows of Trees, &c.'

Charles preferred Windsor over Hampton Court, probably because Cromwell had used the latter as a permanent headquarters, so it contained unpleasant associations. In the eighteenth century the Great Park first became overstocked, then in its closing years fell into decline. By 1810 it was seriously diminished.

LANDSCAPED PARK AND GARDENS

Following the English Civil War a distinctly different approach to the landscape of the Great Park emerged. Charles II and his successors were deeply influenced by the European approaches to landscape, particularly those of France, the dominant power, and the Netherlands, the merchant power already in the grip of what has proved to be a longstanding horticultural obsession. Charles laid the Long Walk while Queen Anne, his niece, laid out Queen Anne's Ride. It is true that these avenues were used as rapid routes to the hunting field, but hunting was seldom still in the Great Park, but in the forest beyond. Visually, these new avenues dominated the landscape, in imitation of the long avenues that characterised French and Dutch parks and gardens. The Great (Cumberland) Lodge, provided the nucleus for a smaller set of avenues, of which there are now a few scanty traces. In the first half of the eighteenth century the great landscapers here were Henry Wise and then a Yorkshireman, William Kent. Both practised their craft during the initial phase of transition from garden formality to landscaped parkland. Both skilfully planted clumps of trees to enhance the landscape, but these tended to have symmetry and regularity. Like many of his contemporaries, the Duke of Cumberland himself was obsessed by the look of the landscape and how to improve it. After he became ranger in 1746 he planted many clumps and groves, but in consultation with men like Lancelot (Capability) Brown, the idea now was irregularity, a notion revived by Eric Savill in the two 'woodland' gardens he created in the mid-twentieth century. Traces of Cumberland's work, notably plantations and waterworks, most significantly the creation of Virginia Water, are among the most obvious features of the Great Park today.

By the mid-nineteenth century there was growing consciousness of the Great Park as a historic landscape. William Menzies produced an extraordinary and beautiful book in 1864, lavishly illustrated with depictions and photographs of the veteran trees with which the park is so richly endowed. The deer were returned from their exile in the forest, but now as an ornament. Finally, Queen Victoria made massive equestrian and military events a feature of the park's life, a recollection of the chivalrous age of tournaments and hunting in which the nobles and knightly classes had posed, looked cool or chased across the same landscape. Military reviews, characterised by elaborately costumed cavalry and other troops, were unashamed propaganda events to which foreign dignitaries were invited, so that they could savour the majesty of the Queen and Empress who ruled half the world.

All the Queen's horses, not to mention her men, are still with us. The Household Cavalry still exercises its horses on the rides through the Great Park, but are now very much more soberly clad. But, as the sovereign's troops, they are the vestiges of a tradition of horsemanship that goes back to the medieval forest of Windsor. One might say that, too, of the polo ground. Polo may have been imported as a game in the nineteenth century but it is a credible substitute for the joust.

Elsewhere, however, it is harder to place the Savill and Valley Gardens within the context of longstanding political tradition. True, they are landscaped gardens in the tradition of landscaping developed in the eighteenth century, but everything about these two gardens speaks of their own time and political space, the twentieth century and an open democracy, in which public access is desirable where once it was not.

THE LEGEND OF FULK FITZWARINE

Unlike the mythical Robin Hood, Fulk Fitzwarine was a real warlord who fell out with his sovereign. On his father's death he had paid a fine of £100 to obtain possession of the fortified manor of Whittington in the Welsh marches, only to find that King John had pocketed the cash but given the manor to another.

Fitzwarine embarked on a four-year guerrilla war against John, a war that ended in eventual reconciliation. The legend places one of Fitzwarine's guerrilla ambushes in Windsor Forest. It comes from a manuscript dated c.1275, barely a generation after the real Fulk died and 70 years after the purported events, long enough to create a fictitious account but probably not long enough to create an implausible or inaccurate representation of what might theoretically have taken place. By this time the wickedness of John had entered into folklore, so any bad-mouthing of John was perfectly acceptable, as this legend confirms:

'King John was a man without conscience, wicked, cross, and hated by all good people, and lustful; and if he could hear of any fair lady or damsel, the wife or daughter of earl, baron, or of any other, he wished to have her at his will; either to entrap her by promise or gift, or to ravish her by force. And for this he was the most hated, and for this cause many great lords of England had given up their homages to the king; whereby the king was the less feared.'

Here is the part covering Fulk's fictive time in Windsor Forest:
'Fulk and his companions had ascertained from the peasants that king John was at Windsor and they privately took the way toward Windsor. During the day they slept and rested themselves, and during the night they went on till they came to the forest and there they harboured themselves in a certain place where they had before been used to be in the forest of Windsor. For Fulk knew all the windings there. Then they heard hunters and berners [dog handlers] blowing the horn, and thereby they knew that the king was going to hunt. Fulk and his companions armed themselves very richly. Fulk swore a great oath that for fear of death he would not stop but he would avenge himself upon the king, who by force and wrong had disinherited him, and that he would challenge loudly his

rights and his heritage. Fulk caused his companions to tarry there, and he himself, having said this, would go to look for adventures.

'Fulk went on and met an old collier[1] carrying a flail in his hand; his dress was all black as becomes a collier. Fulk asked him as a favour to have the goodness to give his clothes and his flail for his own. "Sir," said he, "willingly." Fulk gave him ten bezants,[2] and asked him for his love that he would tell this to no one. The collier went his way; Fulk remained and clothed himself immediately in the dress which the collier had given him, and he went to his coals and began to mend the fire. Fulk saw a great fork of iron, so he took it in his hand and arranged his billets on this side and on that side.

'Then came the king with three knights all on foot to Fulk, where they saw him mending the fire. When Fulk saw the king he knew him well, and threw the fork from his hand and saluted his lord and threw himself on his knees before him very humbly. The king and his three knights made great laughter and sport over the politeness and demeanour of the charcoal burner; they stood there for a long time. "Sir villain,"[3] said the king, "have you seen any stag or doe pass this way?" "Yes, my Lord, one well horned, it had long horns." "Where is it?" "Sire, my lord, I can very easily lead you where I have seen it." "Go on then, sir villain, and we will follow you." "Sire," said the collier, "shall I take my fork in my hand? For if it were stolen it would be a great loss to me." "Yes, villain, if you like." Fulk took the great fork in his hand and so he conducted the king to shoot, for he had a very fair bow. "Sire,

---

[1] A charcoal burner

[2] Gold or silver coins

[3] A villain, or villein, was an unfree tenant, not free to leave his lord's estate, nor marry nor allow his children to marry without his lord's consent.

my Lord," said Fulk, "would it please you that I should go into the thicket and cause the beast to come this way?" "Yes," said the king. Fulk hastily leaped into the thick of the forest, and ordered his band hastily to take King John "for I have led him here with only three knights, and all his retinue is in the other part of the forest." Fulk and his band rushed out of the thicket and observed the king and took him immediately. "Sir king," said Fulk, "now I have you in my power; shall I pass a sentence upon you as you would upon me if you had taken me?" The king trembled with fear, for he had great dread of Fulk. Fulk swore that he should die for the great damage and the disinheriting which he had inflicted upon him and upon many a good man in England. The king cried him mercy, and begged his life for the love of God, and that he would restore him entirely all his inheritance and whatsoever he had taken from him and all his friends, and would grant him his love and peace for ever…'

Untrue historically though this tale may be, it gives a vivid portrayal of life in the forest. The real Fulk received Whittington castle on making his peace with John in 1204. He served him until 1215, when he joined other barons in compelling John to sign Magna Carta. He remained loyal to John's successor, Henry III.

The ecological and economic landscape

> 'The tree which moves some to tears of joy is in the eyes of others only a green thing that stands in the way. Some see Nature all ridicule and deformity, and some scarce see Nature at all. But to the eyes of the man of imagination, Nature is Imagination itself.'
>
> <div style="text-align: right">William Blake, <i>The Letters</i>, 1799.</div>

One cannot begin to appreciate the ecology of Windsor Great Park without some inkling as to the ground beneath, which determines what will grow but more significantly, perhaps, what will dominate.

There are two significantly different terrains. In the northern and greater part of the park, the ground is predominantly a stratum of Thames basin London Clay, roughly 120 metres deep, overlying an even thicker chalk layer which is about 200 metres in depth. In terms of the geology of the whole of Britain, these were laid down comparatively recently, approximately 60 and 80 million years ago, respectively, the silt deposit of warm seas, a thought so incredible as to make one giddy. The castle, of course, stands on the chalk incline, where erosion has exposed it.

In the south of the park beyond a transitional zone of loam, the chalk and the clay are overlaid with Bagshot Sand. This was laid down approximately only 40 million years ago, the deposit of a vast freshwater river quite as large as the Ganges, which flowed across the country from the west. It was here, or rather just a little to the southwest in the early 1820s, that this sand deposit was first identified, hence its name: Bagshot Beds or Sands.

Characterised by acidic nutrient-poor soil in the south, the predominant natural flora of this terrain is bracken, heather, gorse and acid grassland. Where such ground is bare, birch trees are quick to colonise. Eventually birch woods give way to longer-lived and more shade-tolerant trees, most notably oak. Unable to regenerate under oak canopy, birch seeks fresh open areas to colonise.

It used to be thought that following the return of tree cover, about 12,000 years ago, after the final Ice Age, the whole landscape was probably wooded and remained so until about 12,000 years ago when Mesolithic humans and their successors began to fell trees to make open spaces for their livestock, thus creating heathland, an essentially man-made environment. Elsewhere mature woodland tended to be dominated by oak, with ash on wetter slopes, and willow and alder in seriously wet areas. The assumption hitherto about complete afforestation of the landscape at the end of the Ice Ages is doubted now, with a convincing alternative theory proposed: that large herbivores, mammoth, aurochs and other such creatures, prevented relentless woodland more or less from the outset, and that since the final Ice Age there have always been open areas with grass, bracken and shrubs, etc. In East Africa large mammals (elephants) still destroy trees, creating savannah, a mixture of grassland, wood pasture and woodland.

This new theory notwithstanding, it is a definite fact that humans, from the Mesolithic period onwards, deliberately created heathland by felling trees, and with the advent of agricultural technology, a mere 5,000 years ago, began to open up richer grounds for crop cultivation.

Heathland that undoubtedly once existed here has virtually disappeared. One gets a momentary impression of what it once may have looked like from the ground between Johnson's Pond and High Bridge, but real heathland depends on a livestock-grazed landscape. What we have left are the exemplary flora, birch, heather, bracken, acid grasses and in a few places gorse. True heathland may have survived in other parts of the royal forest but it could not survive where there were deer parks, then landscaped areas and farmland.

Here, in the royal forest, great swathes of countryside were allowed to grow wild, as cover for the game, certainly until the progressive cutting of clearances ('assarts' in the Middle Ages) and enclosures for farming purposes. Thus there would be many trees that were never cut but grew as 'maidens' or 'standards'. There are plenty of examples in the park of how these look, young and vigorous oak trees but also older ones where the crowns die back in parts, leaving dead branches or 'stag heads'. This is a perfectly natural process in a mature oak unable to supply sufficient nutrients for the whole of its canopy. It simply allows surplus canopy to die back, a process which slowly continues as it becomes a veteran. As they become older oak trunks often harbour hollow areas and rotten wood. But the sap still rises to sustain reduced areas of growth, and may continue in such a state for another century or more.

These veteran oaks have a vital ecological role, for they act as habitat for an astonishing array of species: hole-nesting birds, bats, rare beetles and spiders, lichens and fungi. In the words of Oliver Rackham, the countryside historian, 'Any old tree should be treasured, for ten thousand young trees do not provide these habitats.' 'Each veteran, a treasure' is not a bad watchword as one walks through this wonderful landscape.

There would have been plenty of boggy areas. Indeed, the Bourne, Battle Bourne and tributaries of the Virginia Stream would have created plenty of bog until they were cut into defined streams, first probably in the early Middle Ages, perhaps when the proprietors of Moat Park, Wychmere and Manor Lodge were creating moats around their buildings, and seeking to drain land so that deer and other livestock could graze more profitably. However, there are still plenty of areas where sedges, rushes and reeds grow to enrich the floral diversity.

Throughout human history, at any rate until the mid-nineteenth century, the area of the royal forest south of Windsor was notorious for low population density, poverty and lawlessness. 'From Farnham, that I might take in the whole county of Surrey', wrote Daniel Defoe in his *A Tour through the Whole Island of Great Britain* (1724-26):

> 'I took the coach-road over Bagshot-Heath, and that great forest, as 'tis called, of Windsor..... here is a vast tract of land, some of it within seventeen or eighteen miles of the capital city; which is not only poor, but even quite sterile, given up to barrenness, horrid and frightful to look on, not only good for little, but good for nothing.'

He certainly noticed the Bagshot Sand:

> '... for in passing this heath, in a windy day, I was so far in danger of smothering with the clouds of sand, which were raised by the storm, that I could neither keep it out of my mouth, nose or eyes; and when the wind was over, the sand appeared spread over the adjacent fields of the forest some miles distant, so as to ruin the very soil. This sand indeed is checked by the heath, or heather, which grows in it, and which is the common product of barren land, even in the very Highlands of Scotland; but the ground is otherwise so poor and barren that the product of it feeds no creatures, but some very small sheep, who feed chiefly on the said heather, and but very few of these, nor are there any villages worth remembering, and but few houses, or people for many miles and wide.'

Defoe did not miss much, even if his assessment stands in glaring contrast with the delights of the Valley Gardens today.

North-west Surrey, over which much of the Windsor forest lay, undeniably had miserably poor soil. Consequently it had an average population at the time of the Domesday survey (1086) of only 3.5 persons per square mile. Take Windlesham, lying a couple of miles southwest of the present Great Park, for example. It was a forest pasture, containing a mere three households even a century after the Conquest. Compare these dismal statistics with the northeast section of Surrey, a landscape of river alluvium and London Clay. Domesday indicates a population density there of 11 persons per square mile. Over the generations the poverty of the landscape and its inhabitants did not really change. In 1822, a century after Defoe, William Cobbett noted

> 'On leaving Oakingham [Wokingham] for London, you get upon what is called Windsor Forest – that is to say, upon as bleak, as barren and as villainous a heath as man ever set his eyes on.'

This part of Surrey was only transformed by the railway and road communications of the nineteenth century, and by the programme of deliberate planting of the landscape with non-native conifers, largely from the New World. The new transport system rendered Surrey attractive to those who worked in the city but who wished to escape it for their labour's rest.

Given our wealth, and given the forest of concrete that surrounds urban dwellers, it requires a leap of the imagination to recognise that a primarily agrarian society saw the landscape very differently from ourselves. Landscape represented food yield, not beauty, or in this particular case the absence of both. Beauty was only for well-filled stomachs, and these would have been a rarity hereabouts.

Looking at Smith's Lawn, the Valley and Savill Gardens, the

conifer plantations around the east and southern sides of Virginia Water, and farmland and sown grassland further north, it is easy to wonder whether any natural landscape remains. Since the late seventeenth century, when a contrived landscape started to become fashionable, members of the Royal Family began to pick away at the natural landscape, planting trees, creating grassy avenues and gardens. Keeping one's eyes open, however, there are patches of heather to be found. Smith's Lawn lost its heather barely a century ago. Gorse may be found here and there, but would have been more widespread before the nineteenth century.

Daniel Defoe and William Cobbett leave one with a strong impression of the worthlessness of the landscape, but that is misleading. Arthur Young, the agriculturalist contemporary of Cobbett, saw Bagshot Heath as a magnificent challenge:

'I never cross Bagshot Heath without wishing I have a very small and very poor farm of contiguous land, bad as the heath itself; even a cottage with a single field would enable me to form some trials from which I conceive very useful conclusions might be the result.'

Impoverished the landscape may have been, but not worthless. Medieval society had certainly not viewed it as such, and made what use of it they could. It is impossible to know precisely how far local people were allowed to harvest the flora, given the strict forest laws concerning 'the venison and vert' (see *The political landscape*, p. 187), but some harvesting was almost certainly allowed, albeit in theory very strictly controlled. Heather and bracken were used as litter for livestock and humans; the poorest people only started sleeping off the ground in the later Middle Ages. Gorse was an essential item for kindling and, because it rapidly achieved high temperatures, for bread ovens. Soft rush (*Juncus effusus*) would have been collected by women, children and old people to make rush lights, a labour-intensive task in which the outer skin had to be stripped from each rush before it was dipped in tallow. Rush lights were still probably being used in this part of Surrey in the first half of the nineteenth century. Rushes and reeds would have been used, too, for skeps, the crude beehives used in the countryside. With heather in such abundance, beekeeping must have been widely practised to supplement foodstock and income. Honey was important before the import of West Indies sugar in the seventeenth century. Turfs were used as roofing material for hovels and also for burning in the hearth. The Bagshot Sand would have been excavated for building, the gravel for defeating the relentless mud around one's dwelling.

England's natural resource of woodland had already been dramatically reduced. Iron age man continued the destructive work of the Mesolithic and Neolithic cultures, so that by the Roman Conquest an estimated 50 per cent of woodland had been removed in favour of arable and pasture. By the time of the Norman Conquest barely 15 per cent of England was still dedicated woodland, a proportion which progressively fell to about 6 per cent over the next 200 years. (It is salutary to remember that both France and Germany today have proportionately twice as much woodland as England still had in the thirteenth century.)

The most valuable commodities of the natural landscape were timber and wood. Today we use both terms indiscriminately. In the Middle Ages there were very much more precise notions about these. Timber meant the trunk and principal branches of trees, most of which were oaks. Oaken timber was the fundamental and favourite material for building. John Evelyn, whose manual on woodland, *Sylva*, appeared in 1664, explained why the oak was king. It was, he said, 'tough, bending well, strong but not too heavy, nor easily admitting water.'

A mature standard oak, photograph from William Menzies, The History of Windsor Great Park, *(1864).*

The feudal manorial landholder would set aside part of his estate for timber and he usually arranged for this to be felled in sections annually or every two or three years. In the Forest here, the sovereign probably delegated his own rights to forest rangers, themselves usually members of the lesser feudal nobility.

Oak trees, known as 'maidens' or 'standards', were usually felled when about 35 years old, when the trunk diameter was about 25cm. Felled timber would be replaced using local acorn stock, to produce seedlings that would then have to be protected from grazing. Oak was *the* timber, used for everything except for a few specialist tasks where the qualities of another tree might be preferred. Such oak trunks were sufficient for load bearing in all but large buildings, such as the larger manor houses, churches or very large barns. Larger trunks were also required for the Navy, a particular concern for Crown woodland for the simple reason that the Treasury squealed over the costs of purchasing the plentifully available timber on the open market.

A tree would be felled and the bark 'flawed' (a local word), dried, stone-ground and sold to the local tannery. Even as late as the mid-nineteenth century – well into Britain's industrial age – oak bark remained important. 'The bark is very valuable for tanning purposes', noted one Great Park employee in 1868, 'The bark of a young oak of about 40 to 50 years is more valuable than the tree itself.' The tree would be worked while still green, for once dry it was almost as hard as iron. It would be 'scappled' or squared with axe and adze to produce a 'boxed heart' for load-bearing beams. Timbers for braces, rafters or joists would be halved or squared, either sawn or cleft, then squared with an adze. Cleft timber was not neat, like sawing, but it was significantly stronger and more resilient if exposed to the weather. No wood was sawn before the twelfth century in Europe. When saws were introduced, there was some reluctance to use them, for a cloven oak board one inch thick was reckoned to be as strong as a sawn board twice as thick.

 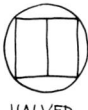 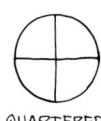

BOXED HEART   HALVED   QUARTERED

The oak had other products. While still growing, the acorns provided useful winter livestock feed, or 'pannage'. Then there were the galls, which might well be collected for the production of ink. Once felled, livestock, principally the deer, would be allowed to graze off felled branches.

The manor steward would allow the tenant peasantry a small ration of timber for house building – known as *housebote*, *bote* being the Norman-French word for a bundle, clearly in this case the entitlement, which varied from one tenant to another. The larger branches, useful for structural work, would also be farmed but often only when needed for a particular purpose. English oaks (*Quercus robur*), which tend to be more common in southern England, are notoriously angular because their terminal buds tend to die, leaving the growth energy to be diverted into a lateral bud. This suited the medieval carpenter well, for he chose a suitably angled branch where now we make a far weaker joint out of two straight pieces of wood. Carpenters understood and respected the natural strengths of timber in a way we have largely lost today.

However, the emphasis in Windsor Forest and also in the Great Park, would probably have been less on timber than on the production of underwood. Underwood was composed of smaller branches of trees, the wood of shrub but most importantly the yield of coppice. Humans mastered the business of coppicing, periodically cutting tree shoots at ground level for a variety of uses, about 6,000 years ago.

During the Bronze Age, approximately 3,000 years ago, coppiced oak and alder were used to lay track ways. Coppice, like timber stands, was managed by the manor, but tenants would customarily be entitled to a ration. Coppice was usually cut every seven to ten years. It had to be enclosed by a thick hedge or stout hurdles to prevent grazing livestock destroying it. Many different tree species were used for coppice, but oak, hazel and ash were usually the favourites. Yew was also coppiced, the only conifer that responds to such treatment. The very first boats to replace dugouts were made of oak planks sewn with yew thread, coppiced yew stems making good cord. Coppiced oak was used for palings and barrels. Barrels were essential items in every manor house,

COPPICE STOOL   THE SPRING   A LAPSED COPPICE

to store salted meat, beer or wine. The role of the cooper was a highly skilled one, using the natural radial shrinkage (you will have noticed this on floor boards which curl or 'cup') to produce a watertight fit. A well-made barrel could handle the same pressure as a car tyre and, if properly cared for, would outlive its maker. Hazel was the absolute favourite for weaving livestock hurdles, for each stem can be split true, and each half can then be woven back on itself without snapping, a rare and valuable quality. Hurdles were widely used for folding livestock. Ash was also highly valued for its springy resilience, perfect for most farm and domestic implements.

There would have been some fenced coppice within Windsor Forest, but the emphasis was probably on pollards, trees cropped above the 'browse line', beyond the reach of the livestock. These included trees growing in wood pasture and in hedgerows, which would be protected initially by thorny undergrowth and then, once noticed, deliberately by a woodsman fencing it in until it had grown above the browse line. Once out of danger from grazers, the top would be polled, i.e. cropped like coppice, every seven to ten years. Most cropping of such pollards and even of coppice, despite the importance of the latter for hurdles, farm

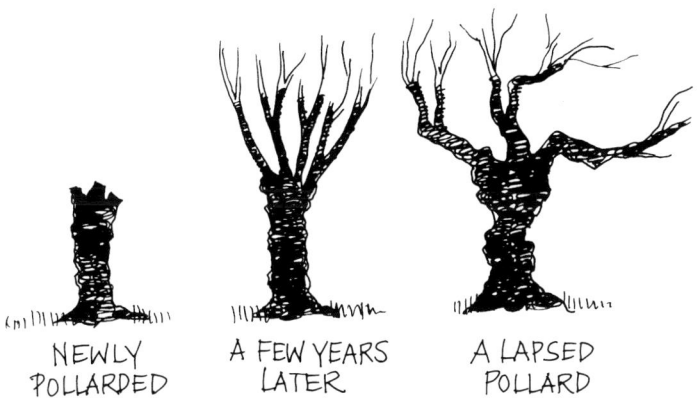

A lapsed pollard, photograph from William Menzies, The History of Windsor Great Park, *(1864).*

tools, etc., was probably simply to produce fuel. Almost all of this went to the manor lord, often in the form of charcoal – hence the frequency of colliers' encampments in woodland and coppice. Like coppice, maintained pollards age significantly more slowly than maidens, prepared to live at least three times as long, if cared for. As they age, oak pollards thicken in the trunk and once lapsed, as one finds now almost universally, they age and acquire great character. You, like me, may love them as reassuring features in the landscape but that most delightful of diarists, Francis Kilvert, saw them very differently:

> 'I fear.... those grey, gnarled, low-browed, knock-kneed, bowed, bent, huge, strange, long-armed, deformed, hunchbacked, misshapen oak men that stand waiting and watching century after century, biding God's time with both feet in the grave and yet tiring down and seeing out generation after generation, with such tales to tell, as when they whisper them to each other in the midsummer nights, make the silver birches weep and the poplars and aspens shiver and the long ears of hares and rabbits stand on end. No human hand set those oaks. They are "the trees which the Lord hath planted".

They look as if they had been at the beginning and making of the world, and will probably see its end.'

Saturday 22 April, 1876

Oaks, both maidens and pollards allowed to grow beyond maturity, start to die back, conserving their energy and acquire a 'staghead' of dead wood, in Shakespeare's words, 'high top bald with dry antiquity'.

Back from the poetic to reality. Ordinary people were normally used to miserable fires, often of little more than dried turfs. Yet a blind eye may have been turned to their collecting fallen dead wood. They certainly felt they had a right to what could be got 'by hook or by crook'. But the vert, the living or green wood, was absolutely forbidden, except for strictly controlled and personally specified rights. The steward would have a ledger with the entitlement of each tenant specified.

In times of laxity the local people would infringe the prohibitions as far as possible. By the eighteenth century, for example, it was a well-established 'right' for locals to pick up dead wood in the Great Park. In April 1765, those living around the edge of the Great Park learnt of a new decree:

> 'Whereas from the Indulgence granted to poor People, to pick up the dead Wood within *Windsor Great Park*, great Inconvenience has been found, and the same has been proved to be very prejudicial to the Breed of Game there.... NOTICE *therefore is hereby given*, That no Person, or Persons whatsoever, do presume to enter the said Park, and strole about therein, under Pretence of Birds-Nesting, or to pick up, and carry away Wood, or any other Pretence whatsoever.'

They must have felt considerable anger against Cumberland at the time, but they need not have worried. Six months later, timed perfectly with the onset of colder weather, Cumberland expired, and doubtless local people quietly resumed their customary activities. Another half-hearted attempt at prohibition was made a century later, an indication of how well entrenched a sense of firewood rights had become.

Today the rules are strict. One may not lift wood or any other materials out of the Great Park. Yet protection now is not for the private enjoyment of privileged personages, as it had been from the Conquest down to the nineteenth century. It is for the public benefit, a landscaped cherished and conserved as royal park and forest. To this end some parts of the landscape are slowly being returned to their largely natural state, with overwhelmingly native flora. Yet there will always be exotics, and they will try to grow where they are not wanted. The problem is greater with fauna. Muntjacs are now a permanent feature of the countryside, extremely destructive of groundcover in woodland. In the sky the Indian ring-necked parakeet (*Psittacula krameri*) is a noisy and growing presence in southeast England, beginning to increase exponentially. They may begin to have a serious impact on native bird species. Meanwhile, climate change may slowly change the face of our beloved land. Let us hope not.

George III and Agriculture

It was almost certainly due to the benign influence of his tutor, the Earl of Bute, that George took a keen interest in agriculture from an early age. Still a young man, he wrote:

> 'Agriculture is beyond all doubt the foundation of every other art, business and profession; and it has been the ideal policy of every wise and prudent people to encourage it to the utmost.'

In 1787 George sought the help of Joseph Banks, already renowned as a botanist and naturalist, to establish a model flock of sheep at Windsor. Banks obtained some sheep of Spanish descent, but these were put aside in 1791 in favour of a diplomatic gift of four rams and 34 ewes from the Spanish Ambassador. These had belonged to the renowned Negretti flock, the finest Merino sheep Spain could afford. George was anxious to propagate what he believed would be a finer wool producer than any native breed.

Don, George III's Merino ram.

The following year he gave a ram, Don, to Arthur Young. It was a calculated gift, for Young was not only an experimental farmer himself, but more significantly he was founder and editor of the *Annals of Agriculture*, a journal composed of articles regarding the experiments and suggestions of a rapidly growing array of gentleman farmers. Sure enough, Young wrote in the *Annals* in glowing terms, looking forward to a time when man would 'pay more homage to the memory of a prince that gave a ram to a farmer than for wielding the sceptre... we see HIS MAJESTY practising husbandry with that warmth that marks a favourite pursuit; – and taking such steps to diffuse a foreign breed of sheep, well calculated to improve those of his kingdoms.'

Young was, as any Australian knows, prophetic. For in August 1804, a portion of 'His Majesty's Spanish Flock' was publicly auctioned. Some of the purchased Negretti Merinos were shipped to Australia, where Merino wool production acquired an international fame still enjoyed today.

By the time of the auction Banks, who acted as the king's 'Chief Shepherd', had learnt a thing or two about rearing Merinos and could announce, as he did in 1802, 'Ten crops of wool have now been shorn from HIS MAJESTY's Spanish flock; the tenth crop afforded nearly five-sixths of prime wool...' But he had also noted Merino vulnerabilities: 'It is... observable,' he wrote, 'that the rams that are kept at Windsor in rich land, are occasionally attacked by this harasing [sic] disease [foot rot], the ewes and wethers that feed on the dry and hilly pastures of Oatlands [ten miles downstream] have never been subject to lameness of any kind.... Experience has... demonstrated... both at Windsor and at Weybridge [Oatlands] that Spanish mutton is of the best quality for a gentleman's table.'

George's interest, however, ranged very much more widely than simply breeding sheep. He was interested by every kind of agricultural improvement. For example, he replaced draught horses with oxen for all the ploughing on the royal farms and thus helped establish a revival in the use of oxen that lasted for 40 years, only fading away around the time of his own death in 1820. Whenever he was at Windsor, George was out looking at the agricultural work, often with Banks or with Kent (below). Nor was he a whit discouraged by foul weather. In January 1795, Kent noted that 'His Majesty walked to and from Norfolk Farm, upwards of Ten Miles, as the Weather would not admit of Riding'. A couple of days later the king made a 13-mile circuit of the farms on foot. Farmer George was no sluggard.

Nathaniel Kent, Charles Townshend and the Flemish and Norfolk farms

I would not trouble you with notes on Kent and Townshend if they did not merit a few moments of your attention. Nathaniel Kent (1737-1810) gives hinterland not only to our understanding of agricultural improvement during the eighteenth century, and so the landscape of Windsor Great Park, but also to our social history.

Kent stumbled into his agricultural career by accident. As a young man he had obtained a post as secretary to Britain's diplomatic representative in Brussels in 1763. It paid a pittance but gave him the status of a gentleman, a status that by 1765 he could no longer afford. But during his time in the Low Countries he had become fascinated by the industry and skill of Flemish farmers whose methods he reckoned 'in highest perfection'. While in Brussels, Kent had met an MP with farming interests in Lincolnshire. On returning to London penniless and without prospects, Kent was asked by this MP to write a report on Flemish farming methods.

Kent's report immediately attracted attention, since improved farming methods were rapidly becoming a focal point of interest for Britain's landed gentry. Kent embarked upon a career as an agricultural advisor and improver. He strongly advocated enclosure of the old common open field system, which if suitable as arable, might best be subjected to either the Flemish rotation, or failing that, the Norfolk rotation (see below).

Kent, who set out his knowledge and thoughts in his groundbreaking *Hints to Gentlemen of Landed Property*, first published in 1755, offered personal experience, 'Nothing is borrowed from books, or built upon hearsay-authority.' He had written that 'Draining is the first improvement that wet lands can receive,' and this he now put into practice at Windsor. Likewise, having examined and admired Townshend's (see below) rotation in Norfolk, Kent adopted it here.

Kent was unafraid to go against the tide of received opinion. Where most advisers argued that large farms were best because small farms could never afford long-term investment, Kent took the opposite view, partly on moral grounds. He wanted to 'enable industrious servants who have saved their wages, or whose good conduct entitles them to credit, to establish themselves…. in business'. Yet he argued practical considerations also. He noticed how well farming families worked as a team, and that those who grew up with direct farming experience also made the best stewards and other supervisory staff on larger farms. Furthermore, while large farms were wasteful of land, he noted how small farms were careful to cultivate 'every small corner' of the holding. In today's world of agro-industry, multi-nationals and large supermarkets, Kent and Townshend (below) remind us that human values like a sense of fulfilment and happiness flourish on a more intimate scale.

It is in the field of labour relations in particular that Kent commands our respect. Where the contemporary and celebrated agriculturalist, Arthur Young, exclaimed

> 'every one but an ideot [*sic*] knows, the lower classes must be kept poor, or they will never be industrious…. I would have industry enforced among the poor; and the use of tea restrained. Nothing has such good effects as workhouses….'

Kent took the opposite view. He passionately believed in generous treatment of farm tenants, cottagers and other rural poor. Cottagers, he claimed 'are the very nerve and sinews of agriculture…. Cottagers are indisputably the most beneficial race

The Suffolk plough, probably used on the stiffer clay of Flemish Farm.

of people we have.' He deplored the savage treatment meted out to tenants who pilfered game, knowing that gentle admonition was far more conducive to good labour relations.

Furthermore he hated the growing trend for the establishment of workhouses. He thought landlords should cherish and support their workforce, and ensure that those who fell on hard times or old age should be treated with humane respect. It was another century before government adopted the notion of pensions in old age or infirmity.

Believing in the symbiosis between good labour relations and good production, Kent ensured his farm labourers could buy flour at prices they could afford. So, when Kent was commissioned by George III to manage the agricultural potential of Windsor Great Park in 1791, one of his first improvements was the erection of a small water mill where flour could be ground and sold to estate labourers at 16d. per stone, 'a saving of at least twenty per cent from what it would cost them to buy it from mealmen or shopkeepers'.

When Kent arrived, the Great Park consisted of approximately 4,000 acres of bog, swamps, rushes, bracken and ant-hills. Kent

The Norfolk Plough.

chose two areas in which to create about 1,400 acres of farmland, which were called the Flemish Farm and the Norfolk Farm, after the crop rotations respectively adopted. The Flemish method was a mixed system of rotation: (i) wheat; (ii) beans and (iii) oats alternating with fallow and (iv) cabbage, (v) coleseed and (vi) clover. This was especially appropriate for the stiff clay on the west side of the Great Park.

Kent loved experimentation. He had habitually used the Norfolk plough, but in 1799 he tested a newly modified double furrow plough in the Great Park, one that could be drawn by four Devon oxen, guided by a skilled ploughman and driven by a boy. George III made sure he was present and Kent reported for the edification of other agriculturalists that 'it performed its works so well and expeditiously, as to be approved of by the Royal Farmer.'

Kent had a failed diplomat and politician to thank for the Norfolk rotation. Charles Townshend, a viscount (1674-1738), had got off to a dazzling start, being appointed to the office we all covet, that of Captain to the Yeomen of the Guard, at the age of only thirty-three. How delightful to pose in improbable sartorial confections on state occasions, outfits more suggestive of operetta than of serious military purpose. Townshend's distinguished career, however, unravelled in the 1720s as he fell out with his boyhood friend and brother-in-law, the Prime Minister, Robert Walpole. At a deeper level there seems to have been a conflict of character, in the words of the *Dictionary of National Biography*,

> 'Townshend, a nobleman of a second generation, was scrupulously honest and frugal, while Walpole, a squire's son, was venal, lecherous, vulgar, and prodigal.'

Walpole's deviousness, as is so often the case with politicians, won the day. Townshend retired to his estate in Norfolk. He championed the sowing of turnips, whereby he acquired the nickname 'Turnip Townshend' and developed the Norfolk four-course rotation: turnips, barley or oats, clover or rye, and wheat, whereby he obviated the need to let the ground lie fallow. A life close to the land left him 'with great happyness and content', which should 'be our chief care whilst we are in this world'.

Townshend probably understood better than most of us how to live a good life, come what may. Between April and June 1711 his first wife, newborn daughter and eldest son all died, the kind of loss from which most of us would never recover. If that were not enough, his charming and delightful second wife, Dolly Walpole, died of the smallpox in 1726. Townshend learnt the hard way about this mortal coil and how to make a good fist of it.

Norfolk Farm lived up to its name, for Kent not only used Townshend's improvements but recruited a labour force from Norfolk. Other staff were sent to Norfolk to acquire practical experience of farming methods there. Kent put his own preaching into practice by arranging for decent dwellings for his workers (see p. 25). When famine struck in 1795 he offered them the choice of flour in lieu of part of their wages, and on occasions slaughtered livestock to provide cheap meat. It would be nice to think that Kent was able to demonstrate the virtues of his values

in the success of his enterprise. Sadly, he seems to have faced
wayward behaviour from several of his labourers. In 1797 it was
reported that the pigs were constantly among the barley and
the turnips, and that 88 sheep had gone missing. The shepherd
had quietly sold them off in dribs and drabs at various local
fairs to his personal advantage. One can detect an element of
deliberate obstruction. In January that year Kent discharged the
swineherd, but a month later he discovered the same man had
been re-employed to look after the sheep. One must suspect Kent's
bailiff, Joseph Frost (see p. 91). With his staff taking advantage
of his good will, one cannot be surprised that Kent summarily
dismissed one who them who had sidled off on 'an idle Frolick
to London'. Kent's farms may not have been hugely profitable,
but they attracted considerable attention for their innovative
techniques in agriculture at a time when many gentry were
beginning to seek ways of improving their own lands.

Norfolk Farm was abandoned in 1871 and the deer allowed to
roam there again. This was, of course, one of the old deer grounds.
With the pressure on food production during the Second World
War, Eric Savill (see p.139) re-established the farm in 1941. The
deer herd was substantially reduced and herded to the northern
section of the Great Park.

Longhorn Cattle

Until the eighteenth century, longhorns were the most common cattle in this country. They were what Friesians became to twentieth century Britain. Longhorns may have been imported into Britain in Neolithic times and were certainly here during the Roman period. By the eighteenth century they had developed in visually distinct regional breeds.

In the 1750s a Leicestershire farmer, Robert Bakewell (1725-1795), acquired some Lancashire longhorns for breeding purposes because, to his eye, they were the best he had seen and he was sure he could improve upon them.

The improved Long Horned cow.

Indeed, Lancashire was reckoned 'the mother-country for long-horned cattle'. George Culley, a noted Northumberland breeder, tell us that:

> 'The kind of cattle most esteemed before Mr Bakewell's day, were the large, long bodied, big boned, coarse, flat-sided kind, and often lyery or black-fleshed. On the contrary, this discerning breeder introduced a middle-sized, clean, small-boned, round-carcased, kindly-looking cattle, and inclined to be fat.'
>
> George Culley, *Observations on Livestock*, 1807.

And how did Mr Bakewell achieve this felicitous result? A Lincolnshire grazier tells all:

> 'Among the various professional breeders of modern times, few have attained greater celebrity that the late Mr Bakewell, of Dishley, to whom we are indebted for many new and important improvements in the science of rearing cattle. The principle which he invariably adopted was, to select the best beast that would weigh most in the valuable joints; so that he gained in point of shape, he also acquired a more hardy breed, as especially by attending to the kindliness of their skin, he became possessed of a race which was more easily fed and fattened than any other.'
>
> *The Complete Grazier*, 1805.

It is nice to know that, judging by his portrait, Mr Bakewell also weighed most in the valuable joints, enjoying ample generosity in point of shape and boasting a kindliness of skin. We would all have warmed to him for he 'was far in advance of his day for his generous anger was kindled instantly at the sight or report of cruelties so often practised'. Kindness to animals was a novelty in Bakewell's day. His gentleness with livestock was rewarded. According to one eye-witness, his bulls, in contrast with their usual reputation for ferocity,

> 'are trained by frequent handling and familiarity of boys and servants from the calf and as they advance... I had great amusement to see two little boys, one not above five years old, get on the backs of them, and with the gentle touch of a wand turn and direct them as they pleased.'

Bakewell's approach would have been well-understood by today's horse-whisperers, for 'he says there is not a thing as a vicious horse naturally, but by improper treatment... if they dread harm from men, they will stand on their defence, but convince them by gentle treatment and gradual means…. they become perfectly tame and are fond of us.'

You will already be asking yourself why longhorns are no longer a familiar sight. Bakewell essentially converted a triple-purpose (draught, meat and dairy) animal into a butcher's beast, producing an excellent carcase. Unfortunately it was at the cost of reducing its fecundity and milking potential. As a novel version of Roast Beef of Old England it dazzled English yeomen for barely a generation. By the 1840s it was a real rarity, except for a few herds in the Midlands, and was displaced by short-horns which milked far better. In truth, we British are a breed of milksops.

According to his biographer, himself an agricultural historian writing in the mid-twentieth century, 'Robert Bakewell may be regarded as a man whose work assumed an importance which has not been exceeded by any agriculturalist before or since his time.' It was his breeding method, whether it was with cattle or sheep (for which he had an equally high reputation), that made him great. Perhaps his nicest epitaph comes from the Duchess of Exeter who, to distinguish him from his contemporary namesake, a geologist, called him 'the Mr Bakewell who invented sheep'.

Royal and Regimental Goats

The goats of Windsor Great Park deserve special mention. They were kept in a special pen in Cranbourne. George IV had been presented with a couple of Kashmir goats by an Essex breeder in 1828. Cashmere shawls were made from the herd. It seems that Queen Victoria also received a gift of goats from the Shah of Persia. During the summer months they were allowed to graze freely in the Great Park, where they were very fruitful and multiplied. What to do?

Fortunately there were some who welcomed receipt of surplus goats, and none so illustrious as the 23rd Regiment of Foot, the Royal Welch Fusiliers, which had already earned its keep by building the Cascade on Virginia Water. This remarkable regiment had customarily been led by a goat, ceremonially at any rate, since the eighteenth century. As the earliest record, dated 1777, states, the regiment was 'preceded by a Goat with gilded horns, and adorned with ringlets of flowers'. Indeed, a goat had accompanied the regiment into battle against the rebel American colonists at Bunker's Hill, 1777. So when she learnt that one of the regimental goats had expired: 'Her Majesty was pleased to direct that the two finest goats belonging to a flock in Windsor Park…. should be given to the regiment.'

You will be wondering what else the regiment gets up to with these goats. They apparently have a particular role on St David's Day. According to an eighteenth century description, while the band plays: 'an handsome drum-boy, elegantly dressed, mounted on the goat, richly caparisoned for the occasion, is led thrice round the [officers' dinner] table in procession by the drum-major.' It did not always go according to plan. While the regiment was at Boston in 1777, the goat off-loaded the drummer boy, leapt onto the table, and off again over the astonished heads of the assembled company. The hint was taken, and drummer-boys ceased to mount the goat, in the words of a regimental historian, 'an arrangement which the goat was apt actively to resent'. However, one must admire the persistence of the Royal Welch Fusiliers, for the regimental goat accompanied them to the Western Front in 1914.

That same year George V presented another goat from his herd here to an RWF battalion. It was accompanied back to Wales by two fusiliers, with bayonets fixed. Self-defence is the only credible explanation. By 1919, still in France, one of the officers recorded the trials of keeping a regimental goat, which was 'habitually stubborn'. No wonder Jerry threw in the towel.

Billy, the regimental goat.

I have my own authority on the formidable qualities of the regimental goats. When I wrote to a retired member of the regiment, he wrote back: 'My mother was tossed by the 1st Battalion Goat.... He had a magnificent spread of horns.' Indeed, in the fullness of time, its proud head was stuffed and consigned to the sergeant's mess.

While the regiment was in India in 1891, it was able to return Queen Victoria's kindness when it learnt that the Royal Herd here was in want of fresh blood. The commanding officer, clearly a man with a future, spotted some suspiciously familiar-looking goats on the road to Tibet. He hastily nabbed three and despatched them to Her Majesty at Windsor. It is as well that the royal goats are no longer here. No one from the Home Counties has the resilience of the Royal Welch Fusiliers, nor indeed of their womenfolk.

Index

ABBAS, SHAH 68
Albert, Prince Consort 28, 52, 63, 90, 93, 126, 131
Alder Cover 98
Anne, Queen 35, 49, 58, 128, 198
Appletree Cottage 61
Argentina 76
Arts & Crafts Movement 53
Ashmole, Elias 133
Ashridge 48
Atholl, duke of 123
Atkins, John 86
Atkins, Joseph 126
azaleas 154, 155-6, 167-70

BADEN POWELL, LADY 41
Baden Powell, Lord 136
Bagshot Heath 87, 133, 203
Bagshot Sand 34, 70, 139, 203, 209
Bakewell, Robert 226-8
Banister, John 146, 167-8
Banks, Joseph 159, 217, 218
Barford House 127
Bartram, John 158, 171, 178
Batayle Bailiwick 46
Battle Bourne 46, 127, 136
Bear's Rails 125, 193
beeches 31
Beehive Hill 53
Belvoir Castle 48
Bentinck, William (Lord Portland) 101
Bergen 34
Bishopsgate 61, 102, 113; Lodge 121
Blacknest Gate 55, 76, 100, 101
Blake, William 203
Blériot, Louis 131
Blore, Edward 99
Blues & Royals 32, 39
Bourne, the 21, 22, 25
Boy Scouts 125, 136
Breakheart Hill 70, 154, 184
Brighton Pavilion 93
British Columbia 162-3
British Museum 89
Bromley Hill 27, 28
Brompton Nursery 51, 101
Brown, Lancelot (Capability) 198
Buller, Amy 103
Burghley, Lord 38-9
Burlington, Lord 71
Bute, Earl of 217
Byfield, John 101

CAMELLIAS 170-2
Canada 65
Canadian Forestry Corps 65-67, 83
Caroline, Queen 106-7
Cartaret, George 34
Cascade 86-88, 229
cattle 61, 131, longhorn 39, 226-8
Cavalry Exercise Ground 27, 40, 41
Cawseway Ponds *see* Johnson's Pond
cedar 97
Chaplain's Lodge 63
Charles I 190, 196, 197
Charles II 111, 127, 130, 197
Charlotte, Princess 36
Charlotte, Queen 47, 92
chestnut, horse 34, 129
Chile 76
China Island 72, 78-80
Chiswick House Gardens 172
Clewer 25, 40, 130
Clockcase, the 65, 84
Cobbett, William 80, 207
Collinson, Peter 168, 171, 177
Combery Hill 121
Compton, Henry 167-8
conifers 159-62, 172-7
Cook, Captain James 159
Cook's Hill 121
Copper Horse 62, 108-11
coppice 212-3
Coulter, Thomas 160
Cow Pond 85, 100, 119-20
Cranbourne 27-39; Gate 43; Lodge 36-7; Rails 30; Tower 34, 36
Crawford, Susan 49
Cromwell, Oliver 197
Crown Estate Offices 52
Crown Lands Act 112, 191
Culley, George 226
Culloden 95, 97
Cumberland, William Duke of 23, 24, 25, 26, 35, 37, 45, 58, 62, 71, 73-90, 102, 143, 198, 215
Cumberland Gate 100; Lodge 64, 99
Cumberland Lodge 74, 97, 100-4, 114, 119
Cyprus 117

DAIRY, THE 104
Dead Sea 24
Dean, Forest of 38
Deep Strood 104
deer, muntjac, 57; red 123, 126; parks 192-9

Defoe, Daniel 80, 206
Delamotte, William 88
Delany, Mrs 72
Derbyshire 53
Dinawari, Abu Hanifa al- 68
Discovery, HMS 77
Double Gates 130
Douglas, David 145, 160, 161, 176-7
Drayton, Michael 185
Duke's Lane 57, 58, 60
Dutch navy 34
Duval, Claude 191

ECLIPSE 64
Edinburgh, Royal Botanic Garden 180
Edward I 134, 187, 190, 193, 194
Edward III 125, 134, 194
Edward VII 45, 62, 94
Edward VIII 81, 94
Egham 73
Egham Wick Farm 85
Elizabeth I 196
Elizabeth II 46, 49, 59
elms 20, 127-8; Dutch elm disease 20
Englefield Green 130
Erith, Raymond 115-6
Eugénie, Empress 134
Evelyn, John 33, 197, 209
Exeter, Duchess of 228

FIENNES, CELIA 35, 37
Fishing Temple 81, 92-3
Fitzwarine, Fulk 189, 199-202
Flemish Farm 27, 29, 55, 223
Flemish rotation 220, 223
Flitcroft, Henry 71, 98, 119
Flying Barn 97-8
Forest Lodge 45
Forrest, George 161, 179-84
Fort Belvedere 81, 94
Frogmore 133
Frost, Joseph 61, 91, 106, 225
Frostfarm 91
Fulham 23, 72, 101
Fulham Palace 118, 167

GAITSKELL, HUGH 156
Garden House 99, 106
Garter, Order of 134, 195
Geddes, Patrick 53
Gendall, J. 36
George II 35, 45, 95
George III 25, 28, 59, 85, 86, 108, 109, 126, 217-9, 222

George IV 36, 47, 81, 84, 89, 92-3, 105-15, 120, 128, 132, 229
George V 21, 115, 131, 230
George VI 46, 103, 105, 117, 146, 156
Goats 39, 229-31
Gondwanaland 76
Gray, Christopher 23
Great Meadow Pond 58, 61, 62, 74
Greville, Charles 115
Griffith, William 160
Guards Polo Club 68
Guides, Girl 40, 41
Gwynn, Nell 127

HAMEL, GUSTAV 131
Hampstead Garden Suburb 53
Hampton Court 141
Handel, George Frederick 97
Hangmore Hill 83
hares 59
Heather & Dwarf Conifer Garden 157
Henry I 187, 188
Henry II 133, 188, 189
Henry III 188, 189, 192
Henry VI 18
Henry VIII 196
Hereward the Wake 189
Hibbert, Christopher 113
High Bridge 71
High Flyers Hill 156, 184
Holbein Gate 110-1
Hollies, The 61
holly 82
Holly Grove Lodge 45
Hooker, Joseph 77, 178-9
Hooker, William 161, 177, 179
Horse and Hound 68, 69
Household Brigade 67
Household Cavalry 199
Howells, Glenn 142
Humbert, Albert 133-4
Hurst Hill 95
hydrangeas 70, 177-8

ILLYRIA 34
Iraq 69
Isle of Wight Pond 45

JACKSON, PHILIP 49
James I 186, 196
John, King 188
Johnson's Pond 62, 71, 81, 91

KAMEL, GEORG 170
Kämpfer, Engelbert 171
kennels 47
Kent, Nathaniel 25, 28, 55, 59, 60-1, 64, 91, 98, 106, 123, 219, 220-5
Kent, William 74, 198
Kew, Royal Botanic Gardens 47, 74, 77
Kingdon-Ward, Frank 159, 184
Knight, Cornelia 37
Kwakwaka'wakw 164

LARCH 123
Larch Bridge 85
Leopold of Saxe-Coburg 37
Leptis Magna 75, 83, 89, 90
Letchworth 53
limes 37, 49, 51
London, George 51
Long Walk, The 127-134; Gate Lodge 132
Louis XIV 111
Louis Philippe 119
Lucombe, William 118

MAGNOL, PIERRE 178
Main Valley 148
magnolias 178
Manor Lodge 71, 81, 82, 91, 206
Maries, Charles 161, 177
Marlborough, Sarah Duchess of 101, 119, 123
Martin, Chief Mungo 164
Marochetti, Carla Giovanni 134
Menzies, Archibald 77
Menzies, William 87, 198, 210, 214
Merino sheep 217-8
Mezel Cottages 62
Mill River 75, 78
Mistel Pond 62
mistletoe 37
moats 22-23, 125
Moat Island Cottage 24, 25
Moat Park 18-29, 193, 206
Moguls 68
monkey puzzle trees 76-7
Morshead, Owen 139, 140

NAPOLEON III 134
Nash, John 106
Nasr al-Din Shah 135
Negretti flock 217
Netherlands 60
New Earlswick 53
New Zealand 62
Nicholas, Czar 134
Norden, John *endpapers*, 22, 23, 45, 71, 104, 121, 139, 156, 196-7

Norfolk Farm 55, 59, 64, 223
Norfolk rotation 220, 221, 223, 224
Norwegian spruce 57, 76
Nôtre, Le 127

OAKS 27, 38, 39, 61, 72, 117-9, 137, 205, 209-14
Obelisk, the 95; Bridge 98; Pond 64, 85
O'Higgins, Ambrosio 77
Old Windsor Wood 123-4
Ox Pond 104

PALES 20, 29, 42, 54, 58, 195
Palestine 117
Park Street 130
Parker, Barry 53
Parkes, Josiah 28
Pearce, William 25, 98
Pelissier, General 118
Pepys, Samuel 34
Persia 134, 229
Peterloo Massacre 100
Petre, Robert 171
Phipps, John 63
Pimlico 108
Pleck, The 44
Plunket Memorial 83
Pococke, Richard 24, 36, 75
pollards 213-4
Powys, Caroline 79
Prince Consort Drive 29
Prince Consort's Statue 67
Prince Consort Workshops 52
Prince of Wales Pond 136
Prince Regent, *see* George IV
Prinny, *see* George IV
Punch Bowl 152, 155
Putney 72

QUEEN ANNE'S GATE 19
Queen Anne's Ride 42, 49, 50, 53, 61, 198
Queen Elizabeth Temperate House 146
Queen Mary's Plantation 21, 26, 40
Queen's Gate 130

RANELAGH, LORD 35
Ranger's Lodge 44
Reeves, John 57
Review Ground 134
rhododendron 156, 178-84
Richard I 134, 188, 189
Rifle range 26
Robin Hood 189
Roger of Trumpington 194
Rothschild, Lionel de 144

round tables 194
Roundwood 100
Royal Air Force 67, 69
Royal Buckhounds 126
Royal Institute of British Architects 53
Royal Lodge 105-7, 113-7
Royal Mausoleum 133
Royal School 63
Royal Welch Fusiliers 87, 229-31
Royle, John 144
Russel's Pond 53

SALADIN 68
Salisbury, Richard 167
Salvin, Anthony 94, 125
Sandby, Thomas 45, 102, 110
Sandpit Gate 47, 113
Sandringham 134
Santiago 77
sarsen stones 87, 133
Savill, Eric 46, 99, 139-46, 148-55, 225
Savill Garden 46, 64, 143-7
Savill Visitors Centre 142
Schama, Simon 186
Scott, Walter 107, 193
Septimius Severus 90
Shaw Farm 131
Sheet Street 27, 29, 38, 54
Shrubs Hill 75, 81
Smith, Barnard 64
Smith, Thomas 64
Smith's Lawn 60, 65-69, 101
Staffordton and Staverton, William 19
Stag Meadow 25, 26, 27, 40
Star Clump 27
Stevenson, Jack 155, 156
Stone Bridge 113
Stourhead 72
Strawberry Hill 48
Swan Pond 27, 40
Swift, Jonathan 49
sycamore 33

TAMERLANE 68
Tatchell, Rodney 52
Tatchell, Sydney 53, 116, 125
Teulon, Samuel Sanders 52
Tiley, John 87
Tipu Sultan 92
Totem Pole 85, 162-8
tournaments 193-95
Townsend, Charles ('Turnip') 55, 223
Tripoli, Libya 89
Turner, Spencer 119

UNWIN, RAYMOND 53
Upper Burma 148
US Air Force 67

Valley Gardens 60, 148-184
Vancouver, Captain George 77
Vancouver Island 164
Veale VC, Theodore 139
Venice 72
Versailles 90, 111, 128
Vickers-Armstrong 46, 67
Victoria, Queen 47, 67, 93, 94, 97, 114, 119, 134, 199, 229, 230
Village, the 52-53, 116
Virginia Lodge 88
Virginia Stream 62
Virginia Water 73-93
Virginia Water Cottage 82
Visitors' Centre 142

WALPOLE, DOLLY 224
Walpole, Horace 71
Walpole, Robert 224
Walthamstow Abbey 31
Wellington, Duke of 114
Westmacott, Richard 108
Wheatsheaf Inn 73, 86
White, Gilbert 75
Whitehall, the Old (Holbein) Gate 140
William I 132, 186
William II 187
William III 101
William IV 48, 97, 115
William, Prince of Orange 36
Wilson, Ernest 152-3, 169-70
Windlesham 207
Windsor Castle 51, 55, 112-3, 127, 132-3
Windsor chair industry 32
Windsor Forest 19, 185-216
Winkfield 46
Wise, Henry 49, 50, 100, 198
Woburn Abbey 71
wood pasture 38, 204
World Guide Camp 41
World War, First 47, 65
World War, Second 61, 84, 126
Wyatt, James 48, 112
Wyatville, Jeffry 48, 55, 72, 89, 98, 112-3, 121, 132
Wychmere 125, 193, 206

YORK CLUB 46, 51, 67
Young, Arthur 208, 217-8, 221

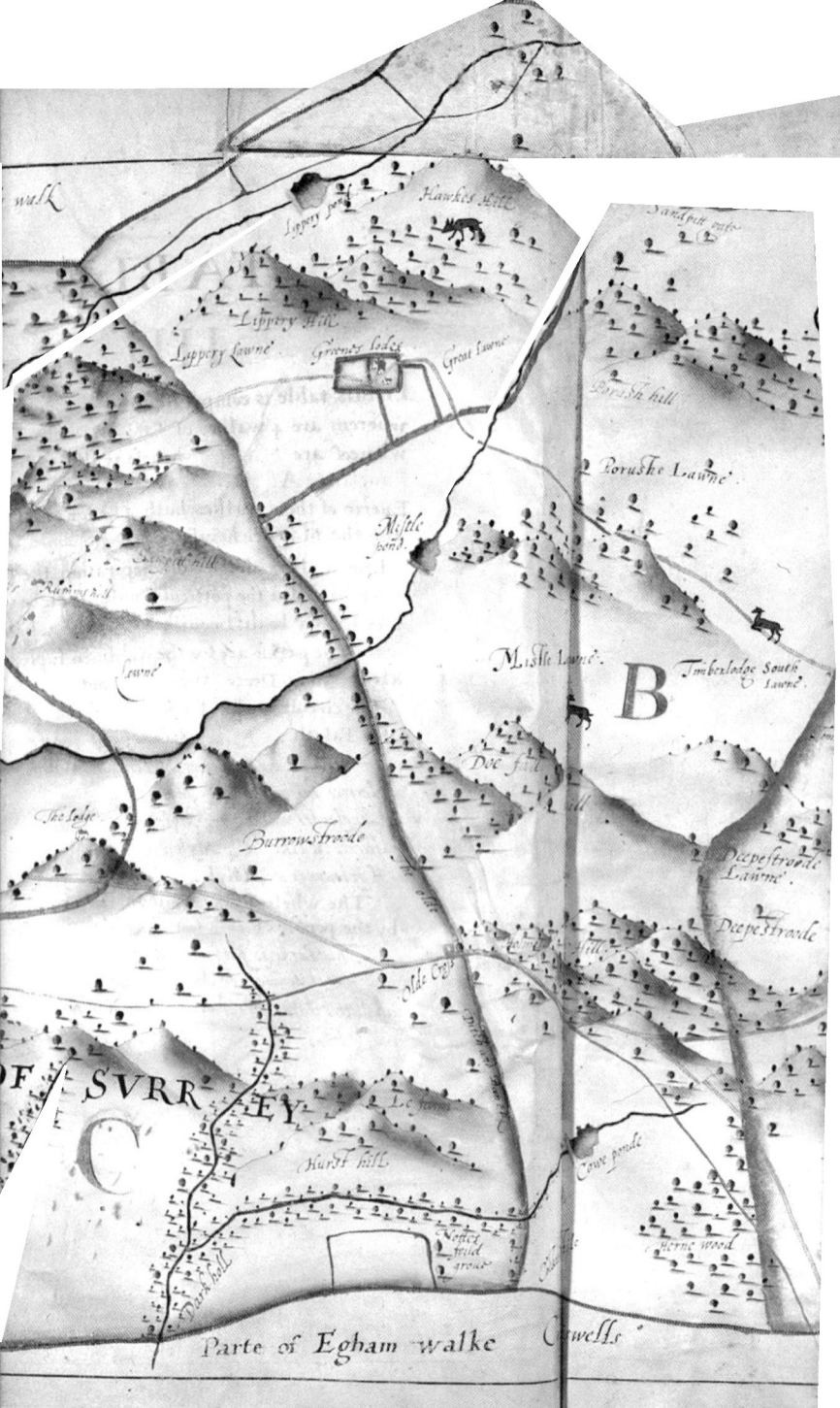

ambourne woode

Parte of Moate Parke

Shaw gate

Well Lodge hill

Shaw lane

Crippmor

The Bourne

A

NORIES

The Standing

HIS

D

WA...

Langland lodge

The Lawne

Beeres Raile gate

Asken gate

Old windsore weed

Part of old windsore

Scale of Perches 16 ½ feett

This scale is ½ myle